Creative Interviewing

Creative Interviewing

The Writer's Guide
to Gathering Information by Asking Questions

KEN METZLER

University of Oregon

PRENTICE-HALL, INC., Englewood Cliffs, New Jersey 07632

Library of Congress Cataloging in Publication Data

METZLER, KEN.
 Creative interviewing.

 Bibliography: p.
 Includes index.
 1. Interviewing (Journalism) I. Title.
PN4784.I6M4   070.4'3   76-54212
ISBN 0-13-189720-9
ISBN 0-13-189712-8 pbk.

Printed in the United States of America

10 9 8 7 6 5 4 3 2 1

PRENTICE-HALL INTERNATIONAL, INC., *London*
PRENTICE-HALL OF AUSTRALIA PTY. LIMITED, *Sydney*
PRENTICE-HALL OF CANADA, LTD., *Toronto*
PRENTICE-HALL OF INDIA PRIVATE LIMITED, *New Delhi*
PRENTICE-HALL OF JAPAN, INC., *Tokyo*
PRENTICE-HALL OF SOUTHEAST ASIA PTE. LTD., *Singapore*
WHITEHALL BOOKS LIMITED, *Wellington, New Zealand*

For Betty Jane

Contents

Preface   *xi*

Acknowledgments   *xiii*

ONE
What Is Your Interviewing Problem?   *1*
    Natural Curiosity   *2*
    Typical Interviewing Faults   *3*

TWO
Anatomy of the Interview   *9*
    The Creative Interview Defined   *10*
    An Interview Transcript   *10*
    Ten Stages of the Interview   *16*

THREE
Conversational Dynamics of Interviewing   *22*
    Empathy   *23*
    Problems of the Hardline Approach   *26*
    Opening the Lines of Communication   *28*
    Some Research Findings   *30*

FOUR
But What Shall I Ask?   *34*
    Opening Questions   35
    Filter Questions   38
    Routinely Factual Questions   38
    Numerically Defining Questions   39
    Conceptually Defining Questions   40
    Probes   41
    Soliciting of Quotations   42
    Soliciting of Anecdotes   45
    Creative Questions   49

FIVE
Interviewing Strategy   *51*
    Planning an Interview:
    a Hypothetical Example   53
    Vary Your Strategy   62

SIX
Multiple-Interview Projects   *64*
    The Nonfiction Article Defined   66
    The Search for Drama and Color   68
    New Directions for Project Interviewing   70

SEVEN
Getting Established on a News Beat   *75*
    The News Reporter's Work Defined   77
    Getting Started on a Beat   81
    Some Basic Steps on a New Beat   86
    Interviewing by Phone   88
    When You're Unprepared   90

EIGHT
Interviewing for Broadcast   *93*
The Extended Broadcast Interview   95
The Quickie Interview   99
The Spirit of Broadcast Interviewing   100

NINE
The Personality Interview   *103*
Uses of Personality Interviews   105
Types of Personality Articles   107
Interviewing Techniques   114

TEN
Special Problems   *122*
Taking Notes   122
Tape Recorders   125
Getting the Interview   129
Coping with Hostility   131
How Do You Know He's Telling the Truth?   132
Pacing the Interview   133
Nudging Hazy Memories   133
Evasiveness   134
The News Conference   134
Off the Record   135
What Are You Planning To Write About Me?   136
The Media Freak   137
The Boring Respondent   138

ELEVEN
Interviewing Exercises   *139*
A Case History   140
Interviewing Exercises   144

Appendix: Interview Report   *150*

References, Sources, and Selected Bibliography   *155*

Index   *164*

Preface

This book is an outgrowth of a startling discovery I made shortly after I began teaching journalism classes at the University of Oregon in 1971 after a twenty-year career as a newspaper and magazine writer.

I discovered that students write passably good news and feature articles if the instructor spoon-feeds them the raw data. But ask them to go out and get information by asking questions of such exotic people as police chiefs and city managers and they're lost.

In short, I discovered that the number one problem of student journalists is interviewing: gathering information by oral means.

Students were, by their own accounts, intimidated by bureaucrats. They said they didn't know how to ask for an interview or how to prepare for it. They especially feared approaching anyone potentially hostile, taciturn, or garrulous. They worried about "controlling" the interview, about asking sensitive questions, and about taking notes.

"I never know what to ask," explained one young woman. "I just hope that the person I interview will do all the talking so I won't have to ask any questions."

At the heart of the problem seemed to be personal fears of meeting new people and quickly establishing conversationally intimate relationships with them. I soon discovered other problems. Teachers seldom devoted more than one lecture to interviewing. Textbooks on writing glossed over it in a chapter or less. I began asking professional journalists how they'd learned to interview. In a phrase, they "more or less picked it up on their own by trial and error." One woman said she'd learned by "eavesdropping on the telephone conversations of the guy sitting at the desk next to mine." Several reporters admitted they wasted a lot of time by trial and error methods. "Experience may be a good teacher," said one, "but it's a damned slow one."

Inexperienced journalists can find scant reassurance from such testimonials. Nor do their editors always exhibit much patience. Says one city editor: "The trouble with young reporters is that they don't know anything. You have to tell them what to ask. They ask it, but then you have to tell them what *else* to ask."

The point is confirmed by a prize-winning police reporter, quoted in a survey of recent journalism graduates: "I remember my first assignment, a spot news story. I didn't know what to ask. The city editor had me on the phone and asked the questions, and I acted as a conduit."

An assistant city editor who works specifically with new reporters has cynically concluded that journalism schools should "throw everything else out and just teach interviewing." It is by far the new reporter's most serious problem, he says.

The need for interviewing skills is by no means confined to newspaper writers. It is essential to those who write for broadcast stations, magazines, books, advertisements, annual reports, technical manuals, and many other media. It is useful to students faced with term reports, theses, and dissertations. Even fiction writers find it necessary. The ones who occasionally drift into journalism classes freely admit that they ought to be out among people asking questions rather than seeking "verisimilitude" in their own minds.

"After all, a man who writes a novel is still a reporter," suggests novelist William Bradford Huie. "Balzac considered himself a reporter. You're reporting on the human condition; it's just another way."

Out of such considerations emerged an idea for an experimental seminar on journalistic interviewing. We tried it for the first time in 1972. The basic technique of the class was simple enough. After a few preliminary remarks from me, students simply began conducting interviews. The first were done in class with observers present to write postinterview critiques. Then students conducted outside interviews, sometimes asking professional journalists to divulge their interviewing techniques and problems. It amused the students to discover that quite a few of the professionals found *being* interviewed more stressful than interviewing. Students heard themselves on tape and eventually, as we obtained equipment, saw themselves on video tape—often painful experiences for them. The seminar proved popular despite its stresses. Within a year students no longer considered it experimental. The Journalism School began offering interviewing as part of its regular curriculum.

This book is an attempt to put the essential content of that seminar in writing. It is intended to be useful to students, journalists, and others who might wish to equip themselves better to face (or eliminate) the stresses of journalistic interviewing. Perhaps through this book we can share some of the lessons the seminar has taught us about interviewing—and about ourselves.

Acknowledgments

This book is to some extent a compilation of the insights University of Oregon journalism students and their instructors have gained through the five-year history of a special seminar on the journalistic interview. Special recognition must go to my students. They patiently saw me through those first experimental stages of the seminar. They contributed valuable insights through their research papers and suggestions. They particularly contributed worthwhile perceptions through their candid discussions—in class and privately—about their experiences and their problems, many of which are intensely personal. Special recognition must go also to Mike Thoele, feature writer for the *Eugene Register-Guard,* who conducted the seminar during my sabbatical leave.

Four other major sources contributed to the content of this book. They are acknowledged herewith:

1. During a sabbatical leave in 1974–75, I specifically explored the interview as a research topic from the vantage point of the newsroom of the *Honolulu Advertiser.* I am indebted to the *Advertiser's* news staff, and to several reporters on the rival *Star-Bulletin,* for sharing with me their interviewing knowledge and experiences. I am equally indebted to some 150 public figures in Oregon and Hawaii for discussing with me and my students their reactions to *being* interviewed. During the nine-month sabbatical period I not only interviewed reporters and their news sources, but I played the role of reporter and feature writer, producing copy for the *Advertiser* while concurrently field testing some of my ideas about interviewing.

2. Like most journalists, I learned interviewing the hard way, by trial and error. Much of what I have learned in twenty-five years as a writer for newspapers, magazines, and a nonfiction book has found its way into this text.

3. During five years of special concern with the topic, I have made a comprehensive survey of the literature of interviewing. This includes not only journalism and fiction writing (where little is written on interviewing) but also other fields that employ interviewing: medicine, law, psychiatry, police work, counseling, anthropology, and many others (see Bibliography). I have also read literature in fields related to the psychological dynamics of human contact, such as nonverbal communication and listening.

4. Finally, I've been interviewed—at least 200 times by students, and by radio, newspaper, and TV reporters. It's the ultimate experience, I've decided, for anyone who wants to complete his education and write a book on the subject of interviewing.

Special thanks to Prof. Karl Nestvold, University of Oregon, and Sgt. Kathy Payne, Honolulu Police Department, for educating me on the topics of, respectively, broadcast interviewing and policewomen.

Finally, I owe a debt of gratitude to several men who read the manuscript and passed along valuable suggestions for improvement. They are John L. Griffith, University of Florida; Del Brinkman, University of Kansas; Al Hester, University of Georgia, Kenneth S. Devol, California State University at Northridge; and David M. Rubin, New York University.

None of the above is responsible for any errors that may have crept into the book. If there are errors here, they are mine alone.

ONE

What Is
Your Interviewing Problem?

Q. What are your views on the future of mankind?
A. Why should I care? I have just swallowed
a cyanide pill. I'll be dead in twenty
seconds.
Q. Uh-huh. Okay. Now I'd like to ask about
your hobbies—do you engage in any kind
of athletic endeavors? . . . .

When you stop to think about it, asking a question is the most natural
thing in the world. "Do you love me?" "Will you marry me?" "Why,
Daddy?" Children are notorious for asking questions. They are simply
acting on a natural urge—a childlike curiosity about the nature of the
world around them. It therefore seems odd that many people profess to
have serious problems in asking questions in journalistic interviews.

"Of the two dozen interviews I've tried, all have been bad," confesses
one young journalist. "Something is wrong or else I'd have improved
somewhere along the line." He's not alone. Here are some other typical
comments of students striving to improve their techniques:

I feel intimidated by "authorities" especially when they ask me what
my credentials are—what qualifies me to interview them. . . . How
can you be best prepared to construct a valuable interview with the
tight-lipped person, or the talkative person, or the person feeding
you a line or covering up the facts? . . . How do you avoid the awk-
ward silences that occur when trying to think of a question that

1

would logically follow an unexpected answer? . . . I find it difficult
to pose a question in such a way that it will encourage the interviewee to elaborate extensively. . . .

NATURAL CURIOSITY

The comments prompt one to wonder: Whatever became of childlike
curiosity? Why should an unexpected answer create anything but sheer
delight in the interviewer's mind as perhaps a golden nugget of wisdom
he hadn't counted on? Indeed, what's the use of an interview if you get
only expected answers? And is it the question—or the way the answer is
listened to or not listened to—that discourages extensive elaboration?

The problem may be little more than self-consciousness. Perhaps people reach an age when it is no longer fashionable to exhibit a questioning
mind. It may well be the junior year of college. Perhaps, too, a time
arrives when childlike curiosity must be stifled in favor of rote learning
in some educational systems. Curiosity is simply too dangerous to be
encouraged. Certainly the act of asking a question implies a personal
weakness: the questioner doesn't already know the answer. The presumed
weakness might better be seen as strength. The questioner exhibits both
the curiosity and the courage to pursue truth in order to fill gaps in his
knowledge. This strength has been recognized down through the centuries
and has found expression in such quotations as these:

> He who asks is a fool for five minutes. He who does not is a fool
> forever. [Chinese proverb]
> Judge a man, not by his answers, but by his questions. [Voltaire]

Of course, a lot of young journalists don't equate the "natural" asking
of questions with the journalistic interview. And that's too bad. It is,
indeed, one of the fundamental problems of the journalistic interview.
The young journalist watching television press conferences perceives the
act of asking questions as rigid, aloof, sometimes self-conscious, often
insincere, and occasionally arrogant or hostile. This must be the way to
ask questions, thinks the young journalist.

It's not necessarily so. The TV format is often so hostile that an oral
history interviewer was prompted one time to cite what he'd learned by
watching *Meet the Press*. He learned to do just the opposite of the
reporters on the show. Where they were aloof he was warm. They were
hostile; he was friendly. As a result he seldom had trouble obtaining a
high degree of candor in response to his questions. The friendly approach
seems especially suited to the work of most journalists, so long as friendly
is not equated with unquestioning naivete. It will see you through many
new and novel situations, and it will ease the anxiety involved in meeting

new people. With friendliness, after all, is the way people normally relate to each other in most situations.

But how, the young journalist may ask, can this friendly rapport be transferred to ticklish journalistic situations? It's one thing, after all, to ask "Why, Daddy?" types of questions in the security of your own family or similar situations. But what of the journalist who must face a potentially hostile bureaucrat noted for his brusqueness and sarcasm? Or how might a woman reporter interview a convicted rapist? The answer—and another of the interviewer's problems—is to establish at least an artificial sense of "security" in which questions can be asked and answered in a nonthreatening manner. In the case of the rapist, perhaps a neutral conversational ground can be found as a starting point. The sensitive interviewer will then seek an opportunity to ask touchy questions, sensing when the time is right. We do it every day.

After all, so common a question as "Jane, will you marry me?" presupposes that certain things have happened in the past that make it appropriate to pose such a question, no matter how badly phrased or how awkwardly asked. Adaptation of the "proper techniques" of social science interviewing to such a question is too horrible to contemplate: "Jane, I now hand you five cards, each containing a possible response concerning your future plans. . . . Would you please hand back the one that most closely approximates your true feelings? . . . ."

TYPICAL INTERVIEWING FAULTS

Absurd as that example may sound, the questions posed by student journalists seem to suggest that they seek just such an approach as a means of depersonalizing and thus dehumanizing the question-answer process. Some of their written statements confirm this.

> Most people are, I think, inherently uncomfortable in an interview situation. Although they are normally quite capable of carrying on a pleasant conversation with others, when it comes to what they consider a "formal" interview they tend to become tense and unnatural.

Does it really have to be that way? Why is it not possible to establish some of the "pleasant conversation" type of rapport in conducting an interview? Another student says:

> One problem is my habit of preparing each question prior to the interview. In this way I may get all the answers I was originally looking for and still not have anything new or different to write about. . . . Although I may allow myself to stray away from the format I have set up, the fact that it is there before me tends to inhibit my ability to follow important leads. While I am thinking

of the next question, I am probably missing a potentially revealing comment. . . . I do not really listen to the answer to a question because I am concerned about what to ask next.

Such a technique could do little but deaden the conversational rapport of an interview. Nothing turns off a person faster than not being listened to.

For every fault students perceive, two or three remain beneath the surface entirely unseen and unimagined. In many cases, failure to cope with these deeper problems is the cause of the more superficial problems cited by students. Silence, so often considered by inexperienced persons to be their most deadly enemy, is considered by experienced professionals to be one of their best friends. Why? Probably because the professional sees silence as a means of getting out of the respondent's way so that he may express himself more fully. The novice sees silence as a personal inadequacy: he can't think of another question.

I get lapses and forget to be getting an alternate question ready should the subject just say, "No." Often in these situations I get caught with my pants down and come out with something simply brilliant like "Uhhhhhhhhh."

This student's problem remains unrecognized by him. The utterance of a simply brilliant grunt is not nearly so bad as feeling self-conscious about it. Some observers suggest that there's something artificial in conversations that do not contain silent episodes. Perhaps they are too superficial, with neither participant taking time to think. It may be that one person is monopolizing the conversation or that neither party is listening. Silence is not the sole problem. Other typical interviewing faults include these:

Failure to Define and Clearly State the Purpose of the Interview

We tried this experiment in interviewing classes. After practice interviews done by students in front of the class, we asked each respondent to state what he perceived to be the purpose of the interview. Over the course of a year we had data on about fifty interviews. In just about half of those interviews, the respondent had either misperceived the purpose or frankly admitted he didn't know why he was being asked a particular line of questions. Such interviews usually result in misunderstanding and frustration—and fuzzy data.

Lack of Preparation

Recently we asked 150 public officials in Oregon and Hawaii what they perceived to be the interviewing problems of journalists. "Lack of preparation," stood at the top of nearly everyone's list. "They literally don't know what they're talking about," said one official. "They're always in a hurry, and it's always under crisis conditions. They just won't take the time and trouble to do their homework." Few busy officials enjoy conducting kindergarten classes for interviewers too lazy to prepare for the conversation. This problem seems to be behind the oft-stated complaint of novice journalists: "I never know what to ask."

Failure to Probe

The timid or inexperienced interviewer tends to accept at face value the answer to his first question. He seldom asks "Why?" or "What do you mean?" He never improvises a second question based on the answer to the first. He simply goes back to his prepared list of questions ("My crutch," as one confessed). The skilled interviewer, by contrast, frequently finds himself asking lots of followup questions. He knows that it's not the first answer that gets to the heart of the matter. It's more likely to be answer number five or six, or even number twenty-five: answers to questions the interviewer didn't even know at the outset he was going to ask.

Vagueness

College students, particularly, have a tendency to generalize and intellectualize. Their writing therefore lacks the drama and impact that concrete details would provide. They're forever asking questions like this one of a reformed alcoholic: "Do you think alcoholism is a disease?" They get glittering platitudes in response, and too many of them settle for the platitudes. But I saw one class pin down a reformed alcoholic. How much total alcohol did he consume over the fifteen years of his affliction? What did this cost him? The answers were concrete and dramatic: nearly two thousand gallons of wine, beer, and whiskey in fifteen years. Total losses: forty-four jobs, two wives, eleven wrecked cars, and "a hell of a lot of self-esteem."

Carelessness in Appearance

Carelessness in appearance is a typical problem with college students. One young woman complained that in conducting interviews for an article on emotional problems of college women, she kept getting quick brushoffs from doctors and counselors. The class suggested she stop her practice of showing up for interviews wearing tattered and patched blue jeans and a faded Stanford sweatshirt. She did, with dramatic improvement in her ability to collect interview data.

Defining Before Seeing

An oft-quoted comment on stereotypes by the late Walter Lippmann suggests that "for the most part we do not see first and then define; we define first and then see." The point is confirmed in large measure by public officials who regularly come in contact with journalistic interviewers. One business leader in Honolulu divides reporters into two categories, the "listeners" and the "dogmatists":

> The dogmatic reporters always put you on the defensive. They seem to have all the answers and they merely want you to confirm what they already have decided. The listener *really* listens. He takes the issue from various angles, gets underneath it and over it and around it. Then he wants to know who else he should talk to about it.

Convoluted or Overdefined Questions

This is an affliction by no means confined to the young and inexperienced. Too many interviewers tend to make bad speeches rather than to ask precise questions. "Senator, your work on the Foreign Relations Committee has impressed many of your constituents here in your home state, just as I'm sure it has impressed your colleagues in Washington, and surprisingly so—your home constituents, I mean—since the location of this state, though picturesque and laden with geological wonders, does seem a mite remote from the crosscurrents of the international scene as observed from the nation's capital, the result of which is to wonder if the citizens here really understand your statement last week that urged the secretary of state to take a harder line with regard to the Delta River situation, which, as I understand it, causes you no little amount of discomfort, particularly on the question of whether U.S. troops should be deployed, assuming that the deployment of troops is still within the parameters of U. S. foreign policy, which . . . ."

Insensitivity

The problem of insensitivity is more common among experienced professionals, particularly newspaper reporters, than beginners. In the hustle of meeting daily deadlines, reporters become calloused. The case of a college woman, interviewed for a Sunday feature on college life, is illustrative. She worried the whole week before the interview. "I stood before my mirror at night and tried practicing all the answers to questions I thought he'd ask," she said later. "But he didn't ask any of the questions

I'd practiced." She'd planned to be "open and honest," but found herself swept along in a flood of journalistic clichés that forced her to give predictable answers to routine questions. Nowhere did she find a chance to express her *real* feelings because she was too timid to buck the interviewer's prejudices and express herself openly. Thus did the reading public lose a potentially refreshing point of view. And the young woman herself felt exploited.

Failure to Listen

Listening is hard work. It is dangerous, even, to anyone who lacks tolerance or who defines before he sees. By listening he runs the risk of having his definition shattered. Listening may bring understanding and perhaps even a change in viewpoint. That's one reason why a lot of journalists don't really listen to the answers they solicit. A woman who had been interviewed by a reporter from the campus newspaper described another: "He was so preoccupied with the mechanics of taking notes that he never listened. I wanted to scream at him, 'put away your pencil and *listen* to me!' But I knew he'd never hear me. He'd just write it down."

Laziness

Many novices think that the interviewer has no responsibility but to ask a naive question and record a brilliant, scintillating answer. They ask a bureaucrat, "What's new?" and somehow expect an answer complete with five W's and the H, all in inverted pyramid form. That's unlikely. It's like a doctor asking, "What's wrong?" and expecting the patient to answer, "Clearly I have a post myocardial infarction." In interviewing, a doctor, drawing on his medical knowledge, listens for subtle clues that tell him what the problem is. The journalist must listen for equally subtle clues that tell him what's new or topical or trendy.

Filibustering

Many beginners talk too much, and a few can't resist pouring out such a continual stream of opinions and experiences that the respondent can hardly get a word in.

Aimlessness

Many novice interviewers have difficulty getting and keeping the interview on the track. Rather than asking a simple, direct question, they become circumspect. Indirection has its place in interviews, but if all you want to find out is what the respondent had for breakfast, there's little point in being coy:

Q. How do you feel about food?
A. I love it.
Q. What do you love best about it?
A. Eating meals with friends, talking, laughing a lot.
Q. What do you talk about?
A. Everything. My friends are rather a bookish lot, so we talk about novels, the new writers, and—
Q. What novelists do you admire the most? . . .

Far fetched as this hypothetical example may seem, it is only a slight exaggeration. See Chapter 11 for a real example.

TWO

Anatomy
of the Interview

Q. Charlie Remington, famous world traveler
   and bon vivant . . . you've been to the
   Arctic and the Antarctic, you've been to
   deepest Africa, you've explored the bottom of the ocean, you've flown hot-air
   balloons over the Alps, you've dated the
   world's most beautiful women in Paris
   and New York and Rio, you've worked the
   oil rigs in Alaska and the balloon logging
   rigs in Oregon—how's it feel to be one
   of the truly great men-about-the-world,
   Charlie?

A. Fine.

Q. Uhhhhhhhhh.

What is a "model" interview? That's easy. It's an interview that defines a specific purpose—a specific set of data to be obtained—and then proceeds through conversation to fulfill the purpose. Some journalistic interviews are little more than simple data processing: "Where did the accident happen, sergeant? . . . Anybody hurt? . . . Name of driver? . . . His date of birth? . . ."

Other interviews are what one journalist calls "a multi-dimensional human contact" in which nonverbal communication is as important as the words exchanged. In his *Division Street: America,* Studs Terkel talked of the human aspect of the taped interviews that made up the book: "I realized quite early in this adventure that interviews, conventionally conducted, were meaningless. Conditioned clichés were certain to come. The question-and-answer technique may be of value in determining favored detergents, toothpaste, and deodorants, but not in the discovery of men and women. It was simply a case of making conversation.[1]

THE CREATIVE INTERVIEW DEFINED

The Terkel concept makes the usual definition of journalistic interviewing inadequate: "a conversation to elicit information on behalf of an unseen audience." The concept of "creative" interviewing employs another factor. The conversation not only elicits information; it permits an *exchange* of information to produce a level of intelligence higher than either participant could produce alone.

Under this definition, the creative interviewer seeks more than mere data processing. He seeks new ideas, fresh points of view, rare insights into the nature of people and situations. He does not expect the respondent to spoonfeed him these elements. He does not ask of the respondent, *Will he say something new today?* Given his way, the bureaucrat-respondent will probably say the same old thing in the same old way. Rather the interviewer asks himself, *Will I ask anything new today?*

If his answer is yes, then perhaps he will learn something new. Perhaps both participants will. The better prepared you are for the interview, the better your chances of asking something new. The better listener you are, the better your chances of hearing something new in the responses. The more perceptive you are, the better your chances of seeing new and exciting connections among seemingly unrelated facts and events.

The major medium to express the interviewer's share of the conversational exchange is, of course, the question. You must guard against staging a debate; you have presumably gone to the respondent to obtain information and ideas, not to give them. But by stimulating him with your own unique perceptions, expressed through your questions, you encourage his imagination to provide rare insights.

AN INTERVIEW TRANSCRIPT

Perhaps the point can best be illustrated in the transcript that follows, for it was out of an interview that the idea of "creative" interviewing emerged. I did not think of it by myself. It came out of a conversational interchange —or to be more exact, out of *three* conversational interchanges, of which

[1] Studs Terkel, *Division Street: America.* © 1967 by Pantheon Books, a division of Random House, Inc. Reprinted by permission of the publisher.

the dialogue below is a composite. It more or less follows the traditional structure of the journalistic interview, which normally runs through ten stages as follows:

1. Defining the purpose
2. Conducting background research
3. Requesting interview appointment
4. Preliminary planning
5. Meeting the respondent; conversational icebreakers
6. Getting down to business
7. Establishing easy rapport
8. Asking the bomb (sensitive or embarrassing question)
9. Recovering
10. Concluding the interview

This interview takes place in my office; the interviewer is a young woman who carries a small notebook and a cassette tape recorder. The name Jean MacDuffie is fictitious.

How many of the stages can you identify in the interview? How does the interviewer probe for detail? Does the respondent have all his statements cut and dried or is there some slippage, or even joint negotiation, in arriving at a conclusion?

Q. Good morning.
A. Hi. I'll bet you're Jean MacDuffie. Right?
Q. Right. I'm early . . . shall I wait outside?
A. No, no. Come on in.
Q. (She sits down, and we talk around the corner of the desk rather than across it.) I really appreciate your taking the time to talk with me. I think I explained what I wanted when I talked with you last week on the phone—I can go over it again if you want.
A. Well, I think you said you were giving a speech on interviewing.
Q. Right. I'm talking to a high school journalism class about interviewing—
A. Well, good luck.
Q. Umm . . . the way you say that sounds ominous.
A. Some high school classes are pretty grim. If you're not talking about sex, violence, and blood, they tune you out. (We discuss the relative merits of high school and college audiences for a few minutes.)
Q. One of your students said I should ask you about your bicycling trophy. Is that it? (Points to "Snoopy" trophy captioned "World's Greatest Bicycle Rider.")

A. I think that student is playing a little trick on you. I just got through telling a class the other day that they ought to make an effort to find something around the room to comment on, a picture or trophy or a book—anything for a conversational ice-breaker. (We talk about bicycling for a few moments; it turns out that she's a "bicycle freak," too, and so the ice is properly thawed.)

Q. May I turn on the recorder? On the phone you said you had no objection.

A. None, whatever. Go ahead.

Q. Oh, and did I mention that I might want to use the tape, in class I mean, quotes from it?

A. Fine. Okay.

Q. (She turns on the recorder and sets it on the middle of the desk, well removed from the line of sight between us.) As I said on the phone there are two specific directions I want to go; your experiences as a professional journalist is one. Then I want to talk about the problems in interviewing, you know, the dumb things you see students doing.

A. Okay.

Q. Okay, uh, one of your students told me that you said the most difficult class of people to interview in the world is the football coach. Is that really true? Were you just kidding or what?

A. Oh, no. No. I'm serious. Well, okay, maybe tongue *slightly* in cheek. What I said was coaches represent the kind of people, who have been interviewed so many times that they know what they're probably going to be asked. And so they give stock, cliché answers, no matter what the questions are. I can't say that I blame them. Sports writers have been guilty of asking some pretty cliché-laden questions themselves, things like, "What kind of season you got coming up this year, coach?" And so the coach naturally gives some platitudinous answer like, "It's a building year, son." That's what gets quoted.

Q. Have you yourself interviewed a lot of coaches?

A. Not many; a few.

Q. I was wondering how you reached this conclusion; I mean, I gather there was quite a bit of discussion in your class; not everybody agreed—

A. Yeah, well it's—I think some of the students who write sports agreed. But the point I was trying to make is that experienced respondents are often harder to interview than inexperienced. The inexperienced haven't bothered to develop a public facade like a coach or a politician; they're more willing to be just themselves.

Q. Okay, uh, are you saying that coaches represent a class of people who are tough to interview? I mean, it's not just coaches—

A. No, except that sports clichés seem more rampant and obnoxious than most. And I also think that on the whole sports writing is the worst in the paper. Politicians and bureaucrats may utter clichés, too, probably do, but they don't get quoted in the paper so often.

Q. Okay, okay. Um, I'm curious . . . is there an opposite side to what you just said; I mean, are there kinds of people who are especially *easy* to interview?

A. Yeah, I can think of a couple. What little sports writing experience I've had suggests to me that athletes are easy to interview, at least when their team is winning. They're open and honest; they're not trying to con you. Young women, maybe college age or a little older seem more likely to be honest. . . . I guess what I *really* mean is just young college people generally.

Q. Young people are easier to interview than old?

A. Yeah.

Q. Hmmm.

A. I suppose one reason is that they haven't assumed the kind of responsibilities that would cause them to be more guarded. By the time you're forty and responsible for a huge bureaucracy you can, uh, you can no longer afford to just be yourself. You are a spokesman, or maybe your real estate business will suffer if you speak your mind, or your wife will get ostracized at the bridge club because you dared to express your outrageous views. You know?

Q. Sure. Could I ask you what you see as the interviewer's main problems, like what problems you see in the inexperienced students you have in class?

A. (The answer is a ten-minute monologue that outlines largely the same problems as those cited in Chapter 1.)

Q. Okay, you've done lots of interviews yourself, right?

A. You mean as a newsman and writer? . . . Right.

Q. Thousands, I suppose?

A. I suppose.

Q. Do *you* ever have problems, even with all that experience?

A. Oh, sure. I particularly remember interviewing the wife of a businessman I was writing about. Wives as a rule are terrific at recalling anecdotes about their men. So are teenage daughters for that matter. Well, this woman was an exception to this rule. She was scared to death, and I couldn't do anything to relax her. I talked with her for an hour and the most important thing I got was the names and ages of their children.

Q. You say women are better than men at recalling detail?

A. It's certainly been so in my experience. Wives love to talk and spill everything about their husbands, even some of the bad.

They especially enjoy telling anecdotes. They say things like, "When you see him, ask him about the time . . ."

Q. You said something a moment ago about daughters.

A. Yeah, well they're almost better than wives. For that purpose, I mean, talking about their fathers. Don't ask me why. There just seems to be some special affinity there, I guess.

Q. I talked with one of your students the other day, and she mentioned some problems she had interviewing you.

A. Oh?

Q. Yeah, she said she'd completely blown it. Rambled all over the place, and her mind went blank, you were annoyed, and she left feeling just wrung out. Then what *really* blew her mind was you gave her an "A" for the interview. Do you remember that?

A. Right. She mentioned those things to you?

Q. Yes. You actually gave her an "A"?

A. I think so. As I recall she had me thinking about a lot of things I'd never thought of before.

Q. Well, she told me quite a bit about the interview, but I'm wondering what it was that you thought was so good.

A. I'm not sure I can remember it in all its nuances. What stands out in memory was that she was sincere; I mean, she really wanted my answers. She wanted to know some views on writing and journalism education as I recall. Well, it wasn't just idle curiosity. She'd been in my writing classes, and I have a bad reputation I guess for making detailed and sometimes blunt critical responses to their written work. I make them in writing. It's a lot of work, and sometimes I think the only people who seem to appreciate it are the very good students and the very bad, maybe 20 percent of the total. The good because they're at a level where they can take criticism and the bad because it's the first time anyone's tried to analyze exactly what's wrong with their writing. Anyway, all this was lurking beneath the surface of that interview. There are often things about any interview that don't show up on a verbal level.

Q. Uh-huh.

A. So she got me talking about myself and some personal philosophies of teaching. One thing that stands out in memory is that I said I don't have strong personal opinions. I said people from my background, lower-class, immigrant parents, can't afford the luxury of strong opinions, unlike people from the comfortable middle class. Then later in the conversation she somehow provoked me or challenged me—or something—into expressing strong opinions all over the place. I was getting damned tired of writing lengthy and laborious critiques for mediocre writers. I said I didn't like the middle-class ripoff among the radical students; that was another. That had to do with my theory that middle-class kids were trying to exploit the natural petulance of blacks and American Indians and Chicanos. Well, that led me to a denunciation of the fraternity system and I don't know what all. Then I think I said that universities are deadly dull places where nothing significant ever happens for journalists to write about.

Q. So you do have strong opinions.

A. Yeah. And she caught that and started asking about it. Well, if I was annoyed, that would be the reason, not any rambling or self-consciousness she may have felt. Wittingly or unwittingly, she'd forced me to face up to a certain truth. So I graded the session an "A." I mean, it's like if your arrow hits the bull's-eye, what does it matter that it's done a few loops and convolutions before it gets there?

Q. The interesting thing about all this is that someone else might have asked precisely the same thing and you would have reacted differently. I mean, she seemed to bring out a certain mood in you. Maybe if she'd done it a day earlier or a day later, even, it might have been different.

A. I don't doubt it.

Q. Doesn't that suggest there's something—I don't know—something—

A. Yes.

Q. —impure maybe. I mean in a social science sense. You couldn't get any statistical validity out of the kind of interview you're talking about.

A. Yes, definitely.

Q. Even an interviewer striving to be objective—

A. Yes, . . . still puts his personality into it. By his questions, undoubtedly. And even by his nonverbal reaction to the answers. His smiles, his frowns, the way he looks at the respondent—sure. It makes a difference.

Q. Of course you can't put a smile or a frown into your story.

A. No, but you can quote what the respondent says in answer to a smile or frown. Writers do it all the time. A guy who knows how to throw a wicked frown can get a lot of good quotes that way.

Q. Hmmm.

A. Which suggests that in large part it's the interview that makes or breaks a feature story. I guess there's a place for what you'd call "creative interviewing" as well as creative writing. I hadn't thought of that before, at least not quite that way. In creative writing you put pieces of information together in novel ways to produce a fresh insight. In creative interviewing you take pieces from things you've read, conversations and experiences you've

had, and you mix them in with what your respondent is saying.
And then you say something like, "Hey, look at this and this and
this—doesn't it all add up to—?" and the guy says, "Well damned
if it doesn't!" He's probably never thought of it before but now
the two of you working together have come up with a fresh
idea. . . .

This fragment of interview transcript demonstrates several important elements in journalistic interviewing quite aside from the discussion itself.
Here are some of them.

1. The interviewer's purpose was made very clear.

2. She demonstrated some preparation; she'd talked to some students
about interviewing and could bring some of their reactions into the
conversation.

3. She was reasonably relaxed, and she started the conversation
amiably.

4. She was alert to what was being said, seeking clarifications and
additional information as necessary.

5. She quickly followed up clues and leads that might produce fresh
ideas, such as the point about asking teenage daughters about their
fathers.

6. By her gentle probing, she helped to develop some thoughts about
the "creative interviewing" concept. This kind of probing is especially
valuable because it shows the interviewer is listening and thinking. It
demonstrates a beginning-to-see-the-light comprehension similar to that
of a bright student talking with a teacher. The conversational dynamics
are similar. A bright student challenges a teacher and makes him teach
more effectively. The same is true with interviewing.

TEN STAGES OF THE INTERVIEW

In light of the interview transcript, let's reexamine the ten stages of the
typical journalistic interview.

One. Defining the Purpose

The more specifically you can state your purpose, the more successful your
interview will be. Both parties to the conversation should know the
purpose; then both will try to stay on the track. Of course some interviews
are purely exploratory. Others, like personality interviews, are expected
to ramble over a wide range of topics.

Two. Conducting Background Research

This may well be the most important step of all, for reasons explained to a group of *Look* magazine writers by the late editor Dan Mich.

> Before starting out on interviews, I would read every available word on the personaltiy or situation involved. I would make notes. . . . When I reached the point of asking questions, I would know what questions to ask. Instead of boring my source of information with dull routine, I would be able to make the interview challenging and interesting for him.

Common sense is necessary here, of course. It's one thing to "read everything" when you have two months to prepare an article. It's another when the interview is one of three you'll conduct today before the five o'clock deadline.

But one truism remains: *You get out of an interview what you put into it.* Flimsy research will produce flimsy information either because you have not asked the right questions or because you don't have the background knowledge to handle the answers.

Three. Requesting Interview Appointment

The first question to consider is, "Why should this person want to grant me an interview?" If you have a good reason and can sell it, you may have little trouble. Here are some standard reasons:

A chance to obtain recognition and publicity.

A chance to tell his side of the story.

A chance to be an "educator" (there's a little educator in everybody).

A chance to clarify positions or eliminate misunderstandings.

A chance to influence or impress others.

A novel experience, ego inflating.

A touch of immortality, with words frozen into print.

Sympathy with an altruistic and noble journalistic purpose ("To educate the public. . .").

Here are some standard reasons *not* to grant an interview:

Distrust of interviewer's motives.

Lack of time.

Lack of confidence in interviewer's ability to handle complex information.

Uncertainty about own ability to give correct answers.

Fear or anxiety.

Lack of sympathy with "noble purpose" or with policies of the medium the interviewer represents.

Clearly your request for an interview should promote the positive and downplay or eliminate the negative. The contact probably will be by phone. You must identify yourself and explain precisely your purpose and the use to be made of the information. You then ask for the interview and take care of details such as time and place.

Contrary to the attitude of some newspaper reporters, you don't have an inalienable right to an interview. Therefore you may have to *sell* yourself and your purpose.

If you merely say (to a teacher, let's say), "May I please interview you on the subject of education?" you deserve a quick brushoff. The task is to enlist the teacher's interest in your purpose. You'll do better with an approach like this: "Mr. Jones, every night my daughter comes home and tells me about the excitement in your classes . . . the time you had them acting out Shakespearean roles . . . your plans to search for the elusive Spencer Butte ghost . . . the spelling games you play. I'm left with the impression that some pretty exciting things are going on in your classes. Well, I'm curious. How do you think up all these ideas? Do any of them ever backfire—such as maybe some people don't believe in ghosts? I'd like to talk with you about your experiences for a Sunday feature article. . . ."

This not only sells the interview but stimulates the respondent's thinking. When you get together, you can be sure he'll have thought of the educational value of searching for elusive ghosts. The result is a more productive interview.

Four. Preliminary Planning

Here you work out details to be covered in the interview in accordance with your definition of purpose. This will be discussed in detail (Chapter 5); suffice it to say now that the better planned your interview, the greater chance that your interview will *not* go according to plan.

And that's good.

Preparation and planning give the interviewer a sense of security, a mental fortress to fall back to if things go wrong. This in turn allows him to depart comfortably from his prepared plan when conversation down heretofore unexplored pathways turns unexpectedly into productive channels. The unexpected turns—the new twist, the refreshing insight, the offbeat viewpoint—are the golden nuggets of interviewing.

Five. Meeting the Respondent and Conversational Icebreakers

In the book *Contact: The First Four Minutes,* authors Leonard and Natalie Zunin suggest that it is within the first few minutes of a first meeting that two strangers make a lot of important decisions about the future of their relationship. How the ice is broken during those minutes may determine how the entire interview proceeds. During those moments, the respondent is making judgments of you: Are you sincere? Can you be trusted to handle the information I give you? Are you warm and sensitive? Are you professionally competent to write about me?

The small talk at the beginning of an interview has vital importance. It is the first bond of human communication and trust. Use of small talk tends to identify the conversation as a human one rather than a mechanical one.

Six. Getting Down to Business

Here you ask the questions you came for, and you listen for answers and clues that will lead to other questions you could not have anticipated. The relaxed informality that you achieved at the beginning should continue through this phase. Do not expect fresh and novel insights and fascinating anecdotal detail at first. You must process tons and tons of raw conversational ore for every ounce of golden truth.

Seven. Establishing Easy Rapport

Even if things are a little tense at first, they should settle down as the conversation proceeds. A good interviewer monitors the respondent's reactions to questions. He is careful not to bore the respondent with elementary questions or intimidate him with embarrassing questions. He knows how to shift gears, speed up or slow down, or ask more challenging questions. He can make the conversation more anecdotal by telling stories himself. When he encounters evasiveness or nervousness, he knows he is in forbidden territory.

But what if he *must* get into forbidden territory?

The better rapport you've achieved thus far in the interview, the more forbidden territory will be surrendered to you.

Eight. Asking the Bomb

Most truly comprehensive interviews involve questions of a threatening nature. They must be asked if the interview is to be thorough. A personality profile would be incomplete without discussion of the subject's negative traits. Novelist William Bradford Huie has remarked that he found the best of people to be 30 to 40 percent evil and the worst to be 30 to 40 percent good.

It's a fact of life. And any interviewer who must explore the evil should make gentle reference to that fact and continue doing so as the conversation progresses. Having laid that groundwork, you proceed gently toward the sensitive area, often by indirection. If you wanted to ask a person about his/her divorce, you might start by asking about some other person's divorce. To ask a man about his business failures you may feed him information about other men's failures, perhaps famous men with whom he might identify. If you had to discuss the subject of rape with a woman who had suffered that trauma, you would not say, "Tell me about the time you were raped." You would edge gradually toward the subject. You might discuss crime, violence, safety on the streets, personal safety, and ultimately her own feelings of safety or insecurity. A time will come to inquire about the attack. If you have any feeling for people, you'll sense when the time is right. It may come sooner than you think—she may volunteer it. A perceptive respondent, after all, senses what you're doing. She'll appreciate your sensitivity. To take you off the hook, she may bring it up herself.

The basic point is to let the bomb down in easy stages, like cutting down a tall tree in a congested residential area. To simply topple it would devastate the neighborhood. So you cut it down a few feet at a time, starting at the top and lowering the pieces gently to the ground by rope. That way there's no damage and nobody gets hurt. It just takes longer.

Nine. Recovering

If the bomb has been lowered gently enough, the recovery of rapport will be little problem. A little reassurance may help, especially along the lines of "You're only human, like the rest of us." Further reassurance on why the information is necessary may help ("It will be handled discreetly, but it's important to portray the real you. . . . By listing your weaknesses, we'll help people recognize your strengths. . . . Others will learn from your bad experiences. . . .").

Ten. Concluding the Interview

Journalism students seem to have more trouble ending an interview than anything else. They can't seem to break away gracefully. Actually the process of terminating the interview is so standard that few experienced interviewers would disagree with it. Here are the basic steps.

1. The interview should be terminated at the stipulated time unless further time has specifically been granted you. Two hours might, in any event, be considered a maximum time for most interviews. The need for longer conversations can be satisfied by making another appointment, which permits both parties to rethink their questions and answers and return afresh a day or two later.

2. You can communicate your intent to close by easy, gentle steps. The first is the very natural device of taking a moment out to mull over the conversation and reexamine your notes to see if you've obtained all you came for. And why not be honest with the respondent? ("I see time is closing; may I take a moment to check my notes?")

3. Ask the respondent if he has any "final thoughts," anything else he wants to say. He frequently does, often answers to questions you haven't asked but should have.

4. Documents mentioned in the interview could be requested at this point if appropriate.

5. Leave the door open by asking if you may call back if you have any further questions.

6. "Goodbye and thanks a lot for your help."

7. Experienced interviewers will tell you that some of the best, most quotable material comes as a kind of afterthought as you are standing at the doorway saying goodbye. Here the respondent, relaxing after the "ordeal," offers interesting anecdotes or observations. The interviewer will listen carefully (pulling out a notebook would destroy the mood) and write down the material as soon as possible after he's left.

THREE

Conversational Dynamics
of Interviewing

Q. Coach, you've just blown another one—
so how's it feel to lose twenty-three games
in a row?

A. Well, I—

Q. Now, coach, you can level with me . . .
you're really at a dead end, now isn't that
true?

A. Why do you say—

Q. You've had an illustrious career—the big
time, the pros. You've been a winner all
your life. But now you're all washed up;
isn't that true, coach?

A. Well—

Q. Come on, coach, you can talk to me.
How's it gonna look in the headlines—
"Coach Refuses to Discuss Losing Streak"?
. . .

A curious change often overtakes interviewers when the tables are turned
on them and *they* become the apprehensive respondents squirming under
ruthless cross-examination. The late Alfred Kinsey of sex research fame
was once asked by a reporter how he knew, when questioning a person
about the intimate details of his sex life, whether he was receiving a
truthful answer. "Very simple," replied Kinsey. "I look them straight in
the eye. I lean forward. I ask questions rapidly, one right after the other.

I keep staring them in the eye. Naturally, if they falter I can tell they are lying." The reporter tried the same technique on Kinsey.

"Now look here," Kinsey sputtered, "that is not fair. I just don't like what you are doing!" (From Hohenberg, *The Professional Journalist: A Guide to Modern Reporting Practice,* first ed., 1960.)

In a similar vein, NBC's Barbara Walters told *New York Times* writer Judy Klemesrud that she'd devised a set of five "foolproof questions" to be used on "over-interviewed" people when all else failed. (Example: "If you were recuperating in a hospital, whom would you want in the bed next to you?" Liberace asked for Garbo so he could do all the talking. Alan King chose Richard Burton "because Liz would come to visit.") When the reporter asked how *she* would answer the question, Walters replied, "Uh, well . . . I don't think I want to. It would take me too long to think of some good answers" (*New York Times,* 2 July 1967).

"I know how public people sometimes feel, because I've been interviewed a great deal," said Chicago's hard-hitting newspaper columnist, Mike Royko. He explained to the *National Observer*'s Michael T. Malloy: "I know what it feels like to be interviewed by an incompetent or a guy whose motive is to get you. When the Republicans asked me to run for mayor, a guy stuck a mike in my face and asked, 'You're not serious, are you?' Now how does that sound when it comes out on TV?"

Even more dramatic is the testimony of Sally Quinn, the *Washington Post* writer whose abortive fling at coanchoring the *CBS Morning News* gave her a certain infamy. The bad publicity over the CBS affair, she said, prompted interviewers to dislike her even before they met her.

> They would come on very hostile, I mean, really vicious. It was like you're guilty until proven innocent. They'd sort of attack me with the first question—what makes you think you're so hot, sweetheart? My reaction was to close up immediately. They weren't going to get anything out of me at all, and none of those interviews ever came out giving the reader any idea of what I was like because I was very terse and not at all open. [Quoted in *(MORE),* July 1975.]

Quinn said she had begun to think about the dynamics of interviewing for the first time after those experiences. "You can put yourself into that person's place and try to feel what he's feeling; try to think what the things are that really get to them. They can sense that empathy and they'll open up to you. . . . It's much more effective to have a conversation than to just sort of grill them, to shoot questions at them."

EMPATHY

Feeling empathy for the enormous variety of people the journalist must meet is not always easy. How can you "care" for the convicted rapist you may be interviewing for a feature article on how people can protect themselves against violence? The very altruistic nature of your project is the key. Even if you cannot bring yourself to "care" for the rapist as a person, you can at least "care" for his ability to provide information that will offer potential benefit to society. Even that level of empathy can be sensed. Kathy Kucera, a newspaper feature writer in Oregon, successfully interviewed five rapists in the state penitentiary for just such a story. She says she achieved an easy rapport in four of the five interviews once she got over her initial apprehension. She simply kept in mind a prime rule of interviewing: "It's not my job or my personal right to make judgments about what other people do or say." She had a further motivation: "I was curious about how a rapist views himself and the women he raped and the world in general."

Truman Capote went so far as to establish not only an accepting but a close relationship with the two convicted killers featured in his chilling nonfiction work, *In Cold Blood.* Following their capture for the murders of four members of a Kansas farm family, the killers refused to talk to Capote. The novelist "bought" his way in to see them by offering each fifty dollars for fifteen minutes, time enough to "make my pitch." They agreed to successive interviews. Rapport came quickly with one of them, Richard Hickock. The other, Perry Smith, took much longer. Finally, after two months of standoffishness he told Capote, "Maybe it's true, maybe you are interested in me as a person. Maybe you don't just want to write a book to exploit me."

The experienced interviewer often finds reason to agree with psychoanalyst Theodor Reik about the compulsion to confess: "It is clear that in the criminal two mental forces are fighting for supremacy. One tries to wipe out all traces of the crime, the other proclaims the deed and the doer to the whole world." Often the persons who seem the most difficult to reach—the bereaved, the troubled, the outcasts, such as murderers, child molesters, and rapists—are the easiest to interview. That may be because their need for communication with the "normal" world is greatest. A. J. Liebling suggests that "there is almost no circumstance under which an American doesn't like to be interviewed. . . . We are an articulate people, pleased by attention, covetous of being singled out" (A. J. Liebling, *The Most of A. J. Liebling*).

A bizarre example of this occurred in Chicago when station WGN called a bank to check on a rumored robbery. To the reporter's astonishment, the phone was answered by the robber himself.

Q. What's going on out there? I understand you got a robbery.

A. Yes, who's this speaking, please?

Q. WGN.

A. WGN?

"*As a practising psychopathic rapist, what did you think of the love scenes in tonight's play?*"

Rothco

Q. Yes, sir.

A. Well, this is the robber, the so-called robber, I guess.

Q. What are you doing in there?

A. Well, I just want to tell you honestly, WGN, I tried to make it the shortest way possible, and it's the wrong way.

Q. Well, what's going on now, sir?

A. Well, I'm surrounded and at this moment I would like to request that I have a minister because I'm going to take my life.

Q. Now don't do that, wait a second! Are the police outside or are they inside?

A. Yeah, just a second—

Q. What's going on there, sir? . . .

A. Yeah, they've surrounded the bank here.

Q. Yes.

A. And—

[The interview ends with voices in the background: *Hold it right there! Freeze, man! . . .*][1]

1 Walter Cronkite, *Eye on the World.* © 1971 by Cowles Communications. Reprinted by permission of the publisher.

PROBLEMS OF THE HARDLINE APPROACH

This snippet of dialogue is instructive. Responding to a few interested questions, the robber not only finds himself philosophizing but even shows willingness to do the interviewer's legwork ("Yeah, they've surrounded the bank . . ."). Given the eagerness of most Americans to be interviewed, it's difficult to perceive the need for the "hardline approach" so often equated with the journalistic interview. The same is true of other kinds of interviews. "Some interviewers believe that they can learn most about an interviewee if they get him off guard and punch away at question after question," suggest the authors of *The Executive Interview* (Benjamin Balinsky and Ruth Burger). "Such a procedure may be appropriate in the courtroom, but is hardly conducive to establishing the type of relationship which is necessary to the free flow of open communication."

The hardline approach not only fails to obtain open communication, but it frequently serves to obscure substance. Former Time-Life executive Thomas Griffith suggests in his book, *How True,* that Richard Nixon in press conferences specifically called upon several celebrated president-baiters for questions. Nixon is said to have reasoned that their loaded questions would create sympathy for a beleaguered president.

Boorish interviewing, of course, can be returned in kind. Robert Tyrrell *(The Work of the Television Journalist)* describes a novice broadcast reporter sent to interview a British politician, the minister of housing. The interviewer warned that he planned to ask critical questions once the camera was rolling. They talked amiably for a few more minutes, and then the camera started.

> The young reporter put his first critical question, and the minister turned puce with rage. For several minutes he flayed both reporter and political opponents, leaving the young tyro shattered and practically speechless. As soon as the camera was switched off, the politician beamed a friendly smile and asked whether that was all right.

Emerging from such encounters is what the dean of the Yale School of Drama, Robert Brustein, calls "news theater," wherein media exploit celebrities and vice versa—"making us concentrate on a personality or a temperament rather than an issue or an action."

Such problems are by no means limited to television. A major fault of interviewing for print, as Nelson Rockefeller has pointed out, is that the questions are seldom published with the answers. Thus the reporter who struck below the belt with his question can rest securely in anonymity while the respondent's every nuance is recorded as he struggles with the answer. Here's a question put to a manufacturing plant executive: "When will you stop this treacherous and cavalier pollution of our rivers and atmosphere?" Is it entirely fair to record the defensive and perhaps angry response without also including the provocative question? News reporters often speak with pride of their ability to ask "tough questions." Is that a tough question or merely a boorish one? Perhaps some reporters have a psychological need to come across as tough cops or ruthless prosecuting attorneys.

One ominous fallout from the tough question and its resultant defensive answer is the Coverup. Since the journalistic exposé of the Watergate scandal it's fashionable to seek Coverups. The confrontation reporter has the best chance of finding one, simply because he puts people on the defensive. They refuse to say anything more than necessary, which causes the story to emerge in fragmented bits and pieces. The more resistance, the more tough questions—a vicious cycle. The mystery thus produced causes the story to come out with all the delicious flavor of a striptease. Conversely, the skilled questioner, creating an interview atmosphere that encourages candor, tends to present the whole picture rather than tantalizing fragments. Lying there in this naked state, the situation loses its mystery and thus its dramatic appeal.

This is why many officials take a perverse view of the news media. Explains one official in a western state: "If you want a *lot* of publicity, the best way to get it is to bar reporters from your meetings. If you want something ignored, particularly something unfavorable, then call a press conference. Confess everything. It will be a one-day story and quickly forgotten."

A classic example of how confrontation reporting produces front-page mysteries is the case of a reporter's "tough questions" of a homicide detective who was investigating the death of a woman. The officer brusquely replied "I don't know" to most questions, not because he didn't know but because he didn't trust the reporter to be discreet. A splendid mystery thus emerged in the next day's paper.

> Police today were puzzled by the mystery death of a woman last night. . . . A detective frankly admitted that he didn't know a lot of answers. . . .

The chagrined cop, completing what had been a routine case of wife-murder, learned two lessons. He learned to trust reporters even less. And he learned to use the phrase, "I cannot comment on that aspect of the investigation at this time." If his patience was running thin, he just said, "No comment."

OPENING THE LINES OF COMMUNICATION

Most interviews require just the opposite of confrontation tactics. The interviewer must be sensitive to others' feelings in the manner suggested by F. J. Roethlisberger, writing in *Harvard Business Review* in 1952. One school of thought on personal communication, he says, suggests that communication is successful when one party convinces the other that what he says is true. The second suggests that communication is successful when one party *feels free* to express his real feelings regardless of whether the other agrees.

The second choice is the way of the successful interviewer. But for his success he must pay at least three prices. The first price is that the interviewer *must listen in a nonjudgmental way*. He cannot afford the luxury of indulging in the ugly American tendency cited by George Kennan in a 1951 speech: "The quickness to moral indignation and to wild suspicions of bad faith which many of us display when other people do not think as we do." Psychotherapist Carl R. Rogers suggests that effective personal communication requires the ability to understand *from his point of view* what the other person is saying. In *Harvard Business Review* (1952) Rogers proposed a rule that has value to interviewers: "Each person can speak up for himself only after he has first restated the ideas and feelings of the previous speaker accurately and to that speaker's satisfaction. . . . If you try it you will discover it is one of the most difficult things you have ever tried to do." A good interviewer does it routinely, often paraphrasing the respondent's ideas before he proceeds to another question.

Irving Lee, in his *How to Talk With People,* reports the success of a similar experiment in group meetings. The rule was that no one could speak unless he was sure he understood the previous speaker's comments. People resented it at first. It slowed down the meetings. Only half the usual number of agenda items were covered. But then a remarkable thing happened. Lee explains:

> A man was being listened to. He found that others were actually waiting until he finished. He felt flattered in turn by the fact that another was trying to reach him rather than argue at him. He found himself trying to make his points so that his hearers would have less trouble with them. . . . The ornery member, normally so quick to doubt, stayed to question. The timid member found that the social pressure about participating was all on his side.

Attention to another's point of view, argues Carl Rogers, can "deal with insincerities, the defensive exaggerations, the lies, the 'false fronts' which characterize almost every failure in communication. These defensive distortions drop away with astonishing speed as people find that the only intent is to understand, not to judge. This approach leads steadily and rapidly toward the discovery of truth."

Truth, after all, should be the prime objective of every interview. Rogers cites three elements common to good counseling interviews that seem equally important to journalistic interviews.

1. Warmth and responsiveness on the part of the interviewer.

2. Permissiveness that allows expression of true feelings without running the risk of getting moral judgments in response: "Oh, you shouldn't do *that!*"

3. Freedom from pressure or coercion: acceptance of the other person as he is, not as the interviewer wants him to be.

It all comes down to sincerity. The journalist finds that deceit and trickery only result in a response-in-kind from among politicians and celebrities who are experts at it.

The second price to be paid for the permissive listening atmosphere is *involvement*. Studs Terkel explains that in the haste of interviewing the working folks who comprised his bestselling *Working* he sometimes neglected the social amenities.

> It was a Brooklyn fireman who astonished me into shame. After what I had felt was an overwhelming experience—meeting him—he invited me to stay "for supper. We'll pick something up at the Italian joint on the corner." I had already unplugged my tape recorder. (We had had a few beers.) "Oh, Jesus," I remember the manner in which I mumbled. "I'm supposed to see this hotel clerk on the other side of town." He said, "You runnin' off like that? Here we been talkin' all afternoon. It won't sound nice. This guy, Studs, comes to the house, gets my life on tape, and says, 'I gotta go'. . ." It was a memorable supper. And yet, looking back, how could I have been so insensitive? ²

The final price for empathic interviewing is possibly the highest of all: *the possibility of personal change.* What you learn from people by listening to them can change your life. "Such listening requires a kind of courage that few of us have ever mustered," suggest Ralph Nichols and Leonard Stevens, authors of the book, *Are You Listening?* "Whenever we listen thoroughly to another person's ideas, we open ourselves up to the possibility that some of our ideas are wrong."

That possibility was dramatically demonstrated to me one day when a former student in the journalistic interviewing seminar stopped in to see

---

² Studs Terkel, *Working: People Talk about What They Do All Day and How They Feel about What They Do.* © 1974 by Pantheon Books, a Division of Random House, Inc. All passages quoted are reprinted by permission of the publisher.

me. "I hesitate to tell you this for fear it will go to your head," she said. She explained that the interviewing seminar had changed her personality. She used to be the worst kind of closed-minded, noisy, radical student (she said), always shouting, never listening. Now she had learned to listen. Once she had begun to listen, people began to tell her interesting and important things. A whole new world had opened up for her. I do not believe the comment went to my head, but it did cause me to conclude, with John Hohenberg, that "no talking reporter ever had a good interview," and to conclude further that it takes an element of inner security to become a "listening reporter."

It is, after all, the respondent's ego, not the interviewer's, that is reinforced by the conversational exchange. So great is the value of this ego reinforcement that, as Nichols and Stevens suggest, "The more you take from a speaker through listening, the more he will give." Even so simple a task as giving street directions to an inquiring stranger can support one's sense of worth. Once the interviewer understands that his own psychological needs must be subjugated to those of the respondent, interviewing becomes vastly easier.

SOME RESEARCH FINDINGS

Scientific research supports the notion that people enjoy being interviewed. One study (Cannell & Axelrod, 1956) * concluded that more than 90 percent of the interview respondents in four major sociological surveys found the experience enjoyable. Roughly three-quarters of them said they'd be willing to be interviewed again. Most respondents found that even answering sensitive questions dealing with income and family relations was enjoyable. The authors concluded that a major element in this favorable reaction was "pleasure in the relationship with the interviewer, which was sufficient to make even questioning in delicate subjects enjoyable."

Applying such research to journalistic interviewing is not only a reasonable prospect; it's a necessary one considering how little study has been made of journalistic interviewing itself. In 1966 Eugene J. Webb and Jerry R. Salancik published a fifty-page monograph that sifts through such research in the context of the journalistic interview (*The Interview or The Only Wheel in Town*). Their overriding conclusion was that the journalistic interview is at best a flimsy instrument for accuracy. They cited several studies that suggest that in survey research the answers change in accordance with who's asking the questions. A black or Oriental interviewer tends to get more socially acceptable answers than a white

---

* See Bibliography for full citations.

when discussing racial issues. A Jewish-looking interviewer with a Jewish name finds more often than a non-Jewish interviewer that people approve of Jews in government.

One of the earliest studies of this type (Rice, 1929) remains among the most dramatic. The study compared the findings of two interviewers who were attempting to learn why a group of welfare applicants had declined to a skid road and flophouse existence. One interviewer consistently found overindulgence in liquor a prime reason for their downfall. The other more often found social and industrial conditions to be the cause. The reason for the disparity was explained by what Rice called "contagious bias." The first interviewer was a prohibitionist. The second was a socialist.

Equally dramatic is evidence that a respondent's ego can intrude on accuracy. A group of college women were interviewed about their "love relationships" (Ellis, 1947). A year later the same women were asked substantially the same questions via anonymous questionnaires. The results were startling. Twenty-nine women had told interviewers that the men they loved were "very good looking." A year later only two of them did so in the questionnaire—all the rest reported a lower level of physical attractiveness. Did the men's looks deteriorate that much in a year? Or did the women's candor improve in the nonthreatening anonymity of the questionnaire?

Other studies have suggested that "verbal conditioning" can have a dramatic effect on the behavior of an interviewee. Through a system of subtle verbal and nonverbal rewards and punishments, people can be encouraged to use or avoid certain words or to say or do things in certain ways. These subtle cues are precisely the same as those used by the interviewer: "good," "okay," "I see," "hm-mmm," etc., or nonverbal cues such as smiles, nods, leaning forward in one's chair—or the negative frowns, shaking of head, or "huh-uh," and so forth.

So powerful is this subtle stimulus that a legendary story suggests that a professor who paced a lot while lecturing was nonverbally cued to deliver his lecture standing motionless in a corner of the lecture hall. By prearrangement, students gave positive cues when he paced toward the corner (smiles, nods, rapt attention, alert posture), and negative cues when he paced away (dropping pencils, shuffling through pages, gazing away, and similar signs of inattention).

You needn't read far in such research before concluding with Webb and Salancik that the interview is a sensitive and fragile instrument, subject to unscrupulous manipulation by insensitive journalists. The authors take sharp issue with texts advocating the hardline approach.

> Our findings run counter to those commonly offered for journalists. A leading text in interpretative reporting argues that "the reporter should realize at all times he has a powerful organization, his news-

paper, in back of him. If he 'curls up' and permits himself to be browbeaten, he fails in his duty to his editor." In another spot the same author advises, "Inspire confidence and even awe by directness in speech." Now it might do the reporter's ego a great deal of good to have someone stand in awe before him, but what confident, direct speech does for the completeness and accuracy of the information this cocky interviewer extracts is open to question. The [research] evidence and idea of role suggest less attention to creating an impression of omnipotence would be advisable.

Although common sense and sensitivity to human relationships might lead the interviewer to the same conclusion, research findings provide valuable support for the open-minded, nonjudgmental, low-profile approach to interviewing. Here are some other thoughts, culled from research literature, that may be of interest to the journalist.

Nonverbal Communication

What is one to think when a wife tells her husband, "You lousy bum!" but does so with a smile, a loving caress, and a tone of voice suggesting something other than what the words say? Albert Mehrabian in his book *Silent Messages* cites a variety of studies suggesting that people are more inclined to believe the tone of voice and the nonverbal cues. In general, he says, "a person's nonverbal behavior has more bearing than his words on communicating feelings or attitudes to others." He has devised a formula:

Total feelings $= 7\%$ verbal feeling $+ 38\%$ vocal feeling $+ 55\%$ facial feeling

Positive feelings about another person, says Mehrabian, are communicated nonverbally by leaning forward, facing the person directly, touching, standing close, eye contact, relaxed posture. Negative feelings are conveyed by the opposites: leaning away or turning to one side as if ready to leave, avoiding eye contact, rigid posture.

Space and Setting

Mehrabian and others suggest that the closer two people are—and the fewer barriers, such as desks and tables, between them—the more positive the contact and the more that is communicated. Edward T. Hall *(The Hidden Dimension)* discusses the "dynamism of space" and suggests that the distance between people depends on what action is about to take place; actions can range from lovemaking to taking flight for one's safety. Hall lists four categories of personal distance and divides each into a "close" and "far" phase: Intimate distance (up to eighteen inches apart), personal distance (eighteen to forty-eight inches), social distance (four to twelve feet), and public distance (twelve feet and beyond).

Judging from such discussion, the interviewer should seek informal settings for interviews, preferably not across a desk (talking "around the corner" of a desk or table is a workable compromise). He should seek as close a proximity as will allow the conversation to proceed uninhibited, probably the near side of "social distance."

FOUR

But What Shall I Ask?

Q. Princess, if it's not too personal, can you
tell me why you've never married? Are
you just not interested in men or what?

A. *Not interested?* Young man, I'll have you
know that I've had no fewer than thirty-
three lovers in the past twenty years!

Q. Ummm . . . ah . . . (blushes).

A. So! You didn't expect such candor, and
now you're at a loss for words. It seems
they didn't teach you in journalism school
to cope with real life!

Questions are like carpenters' tools. Some are heavy and gross, the sledge-
hammers in the interviewer's toolbox. Others are sharp and precise like
razors; some are smooth like paintbrushes for spreading varnish. The
skilled interviewer has types of questions neatly organized in his mind.
He knows that some types are used when first meeting his respondent,
others when helping him to relax and talk anecdotally. Still others can
gently pry to draw out information. He knows not to use a sledgehammer
question on a troubled young girl who has witnessed a tragedy, of course,
and he knows how to devise second or third questions based on the answer
to the first. He knows, too, that silence or a raised eyebrow can often be
the most effective "question" of all.

One basic interviewing concept is that the nature of the question
usually dictates the nature of the answer. "Ask a dumb question, get a
dumb answer," says the proverb. By contrast, brilliant questions beget
brilliant answers. Offbeat questions draw offbeat answers. If you want
answers with fresh insight, try bringing fresh insight into your questions.

For colorful quotes, try phrasing your questions more colorfully. There's one big difference between questions and carpenters' tools. Questions aren't patented, ready made, waiting in a toolbox. They must be adapted to the topic at hand and to the respondent's personality. Often they must be forged on the spot.

But questions can be placed into rough categories—nine have been chosen here—for analysis and discussion. (For another classification of ten question types, see Stanley Payne's *The Art of Asking Questions,* Chapter 3.) These categories represent the needs of a comprehensive nonfiction article. The article must have a framework of philosophical bones, that is, a message or theme or moral. *Conceptually defining* questions help to meet this need by drawing out the fundamentals. The article also needs "flesh and blood"—dramatic anecdotes and colorful quotes—for enjoyable reading. *Anecdote-soliciting* and *quote-soliciting* questions fill this need. The article must have clarity through concrete and specific detail obtained through *factual, numerically defining,* and *probe* questions. Finally, the best of articles seem to provide something extra—touches of creative imagination and rich insight—that makes them stimulating and significant. *Creative* questions, which call forth creative answers, can help to provide this bonus. Two other categories cited here, *opening* and *filter* questions, are designed to orient the interview itself, though of course they may produce usable material as a by-product.

OPENING QUESTIONS

Opening questions come in two categories, *icebreakers* and *first moves.* They may be the most important questions you'll ask because they perform the crucial function of setting the tone of the interview. First impressions count. Your opening questions quickly establish you as an intelligent, open-minded professional journalist—or as a bumbling amateur. They demonstrate that you've done your homework—or that you haven't. They establish the interview as potentially stimulatng—or as a hopeless bore.

Icebreakers

More than simple etiquette, these questions or comments establish the first tentative lines of communication, like the first light lines thrown by a docking ship. Icebreakers must be fitted to the situation and the person. Here are some typical examples:

1. *Comment or inquiry about a personal effect.* "That's an interesting golfing trophy, Senator Doe. . . ." "I see you're wearing a smilie button, Mr. Big; any special significance to that? . . ." "What a splendid view from your office window!"

2. Use of respondent's name. People like to hear their names used—and pronounced correctly. If the name is unusual, get someone to pronounce it for you beforehand. One reporter succeeded in interviewing an infamous British wife-murderer where many others had failed. The murderer's name was Sleighter, and reporters pronounced it Slay-ter. The successful reporter had taken the trouble to learn the correct pronunciation: Slick-ter.

3. Talk of current events or weather. You can prepare for this by reading the morning paper in search of items specifically of interest to your respondent: legal news when interviewing a lawyer or crime news when interviewing a police chief.

4. Talk of mutual interests or acquaintances. "Your friend, Mrs. Eberle, says hello. . . ." "I hear you're a mountain climber, Mr. Big: I guess we must have been on Mt. Rainier about the same time last summer. . . ." "Your wife said to be sure to ask you about last Friday's golf game. . . ."

5. Subtle provocations. You amiably tell a women's liberationist that she's beautiful. You confide to an FBI agent your disappointment that he doesn't look like Ephrem Zimbalist, Jr. Your tone is jocular and you're smiling. What happens to the interview now? It's a gamble, but the winner's reward is the prospect of adding élan to the conversation. It is particularly effective with a person who has been interviewed a lot. It tells him that *this* conversation might not be routinely boring. Occasionally the provocation misfires. What then? You slug it out and/or apologize. The air is cleared, mutual understanding is gained, and the interview proceeds, usually none the worse for the experience—often better. The episode can have a salutary effect. In a quarter century of uttering such cavalier remarks, I personally have had only one misfortune. A college dean of women whom I interviewed while she visited a military base froze into an iceberg when I asked this question: "Dean, does your interest in barbed wire defense perimeters here at Fort Lewis have anything to do with the need to protect the women's dorms from the onslaughts of college men?" She never thawed.

First Moves

If you were interviewing, say, a legislator for a feature story about his fight to ban billboards and could ask only one question, what would it be? Is there a question that encourages lengthy replies with only your smiles and nods for encouragement? Yes. It's "Start at the beginning and tell me. . . ."

"Senator, how did it all begin—how did you first get involved in this fight against billboards on the highways?" It's an appealing question. It enables the respondent to put things in perspective and tell the "whole story," a rare opportunity. Once started, he rolls forward, following a natural inclination to bring you up to date.

TV's Barbara Walters once rescued Aristotle Onassis in his pre-Jackie days from a boring press conference by asking, "Tell me, Mr. Onassis, you're so successful—not just in shipping and airlines but in other industries too—I wonder, how did you begin? What was your very first job?" Onassis was delighted; he talked at length about himself and wound up inviting Barbara to continue the interview aboard his yacht with the sly warning, "I guarantee you will get *on* the yacht, but I don't guarantee that you will get *off*" (Walters, *How to Talk with Practically Anybody about Practically Anything*).

This opening question has other advantages for the interviewer. Beginnings are often dramatic and make good copy. They also represent the simplest conceptual stage of any situation, thus becoming a foundation for the interviewer's understanding of the complexities to follow. Of course, that's not the only possibility for openers. Whatever line of questioning you choose, it should fulfill the purpose of opening questions: to start the conversation in an appetizing and highly ego-supportive manner. Here are some other possibilities:

1. Continuing the icebreaker conversation. If the icebreaker touches on things you want to know about, why not continue? You started off talking about mountain climbing, and the subject is certainly pertinent to your personality article. So go ahead. Later you can move on to other topics.

2. Report what people are saying about him. People love to hear about themselves. You're sure to gain attention by selecting for openers those friendly, ego-supportive items that direct the conversation into productive channels. Not everything has to be flattering, of course: Thus:

> Q. Senator, I've talked to a lot of people, and I've heard good and bad things about your fight against billboards.
> A. Oh?
> Q. Which do you want first, the good or the bad?
> A. How about the bad?
> Q. Okay, your campaign manager tells me he thinks your fight will cost you a lot of votes in the next election—what do *you* think?

3. Defusing hostility. Perhaps your newspaper has opposed the senator's position. Your first questions should be phrased carefully so as to suggest your open-minded tolerance. Don't ask, "Senator, why do you carry on this long, fruitless vendetta against billboards at the expense of other, more meaningful programs?" You could approach the same question a step at a time with more ego-reinforcing kinds of questions. "Senator, it must take terrific courage to carry on this battle. . . ." Or you could ask a funneling series: "Senator, you've been a fighter throughout your career. . . . Which fights do you feel you've won? . . . Which have you lost? . . . What about billboards?" (More on hostility in Chapter 9.)

4. Humorous or ironic. Oriana Fallaci, the famed Italian newspaper columnist, once opened an interview with a bullfighter by suggesting that when she sees a bullfight, her sympathies are all with the bull. The response? *"Caramba!* Mine too!" A reporter, discussing the "poverty" of today's college students, opened an interview with a young woman by asking her to list the price of each item of clothing she was wearing. Her comments while enveloped in more than a hundred dollars worth of apparel had a strangely ironic ring.

FILTER QUESTIONS

Filter questions are designed to establish a respondent's qualifications for answering. A "witness" to a tragedy gives you all kinds of details, but then you learn he hadn't actually seen the tragedy. You're getting second-hand information. A simple filter question—"Where were you when the tornado struck?"—would have avoided this wasted time.

The filter question needs to be asked whenever the respondent talks on a subject for which he has unknown credentials. You're interviewing a homicide detective, let's say. You know he has good credentials for talking about murder, but now you want to ask him about runaway kids. Ask a filter question first: "Lieutenant, have you had experiences with runaway children?" Filter questions have a curious impact on conversational rapport. They tend to enhance rapport with highly qualified respondents and weaken it with poorly qualified. The reason is obvious. To be asked questions that qualify you as an authority is ego-gratifying. To be asked questions that expose your lack of knowledge is humiliating. One important exception to this rule: People who have had a lot written about them resent being asked questions that could more easily be answered by reading the library clips.

ROUTINELY FACTUAL QUESTIONS

Nothing is quite so effective as the newswriter's 5-W concept for outlining the factual dimensions of any situation under discussion: *Who, What, When, Where, Why,* and *How.* They work for novelists and poets, too, as Rudyard Kipling demonstrated in a famous verse.

I keep six honest serving-men
(They taught me all I knew).
Their names are what and why and when
and how and where and who.

The journalist employs these men in almost any situation: *What* happened? *Where* and *when* did it happen? *Who* was involved? *How* did it happen? The *why* is more complex and really belongs in the "conceptually defining" category of questions.

These questions are often necessary to lay a foundation of knowledge before you can proceed with more complex questions. A news reporter encounters a group of pickets in front of City Hall. You find the person who seems to be in charge and ask foundation kinds of questions: What is the purpose of the picketing? . . . What organization do you represent? . . . Who are your leaders? . . . What city official are you trying to reach? . . . What do you want to say to that official? . . . How long have you been here? . . . How long do you plan to stay? . . . What points are at issue? . . . What other ways have you sought to air these points? . . . What will you do if unsuccessful here at City Hall? . . .

Routine questions also make good opening questions. They are non-threatening. An inexperienced respondent has no trouble coping with questions like, "How long have you lived here in River City?"

NUMERICALLY DEFINING QUESTIONS

Numbers help to define a person or situation. Baseball players have .314 batting averages, halfbacks gain 7.4 yards-per-carry, coaches have 104-76-4 won-lost-tied records. Statistics dominate athletics, business, finance, and beauty contests to an unfortunate degree but seem largely ignored everywhere else. The increasing use of pocket calculators will surely change that.

Other people accumulate numerical records, too. A mountain climber has totaled 77 peaks, 283 glacier traverses, and 21 days holed up in snow caves waiting out sudden mountain blizzards. The reformed alcoholic has a lifetime record of almost 2,000 gallons of booze consumed. In one recent news interview, a call girl was able to describe her "clients" statistically: 40 percent were white middle-class businessmen; their average age was 41; they came in 12 categories, such as "freaks," "virgin busters," "lovers," and "those who want only talk and sex therapy."

Such detail is concrete, dramatic, and often overlooked. The interview, admittedly, is a poor way of compiling such information. But frequently it is the only way. Respondents can, with prodding, work out rough numbers that define their activities and their lives. How many miles has the postman walked in his lifetime? How many contracts has the business-man signed in a fifty-year career? How many thousands of students has the retiring teacher flunked (or presented with "A" grades)? It sounds more awesome than it is. The reformed alcoholic arrived at his two thousand gallons simply by estimating he drank two bottles of wine or a six-pack of beer every day for fifteen years.

CONCEPTUALLY DEFINING QUESTIONS

Sometimes a conceptually defining question can be asked in one word: *Why?* At least that's the basis of the philosophical fundamentals that you hope to draw out. Simple. The question, however, implies trying to understand the answer, and *that* can be complex indeed. Not only is the answer possibly complicated, but you're never sure that any answer given equates with truth. Truth comes at many levels. So do "coverups," and nowhere is the coverup more apparent than when you begin to deal with motivational fundamentals. You ask your neighbor why he bought a new Oldsmobile, and he replies, "Because I like Oldsmobiles better than Buicks." You can settle for that or you can peel away successive layers of coverup until you get somewhere close to reality: He is an obsequious man who hopes through the purchase of an expensive car to gain self-confidence, the admiration of his neighbors, and the respect of his wife and teenage kids.

No formula exists for asking "Why?" except to suggest that just asking is not enough. You have to create the right atmosphere and rapport to encourage candid answers, and you have to listen with intelligence, percep-tion, and sympathetic understanding.

One pattern, if not formula, for this conceptual level of interviewing has been suggested by Professor LaRue Gilleland of the University of Nevada. It's called *GOSS,* an acronym for Goals-Obstacles-Solution-Start. It can be applied to a wide variety of interviews. It is based on the principle that most of life—including that of bureaucratic agencies as well as human beings—involves reaching for *goals,* not all of them within one's grasp. You invariably find *obstacles* blocking access to these goals. But possible *solutions* exist. The final S suggests that interviews might profitably go back to the beginning for background information.

You could apply GOSS to an interview with the mayor about a proposed new city hall ("What goals does the city seek through building a new city hall? . . . What stands in the way of our doing it?"). You could apply it to a personality profile ("Professor Jones, what do you hope to achieve through your teaching and research? . . . Is there anything stop-ping you from accomplishing your goals? . . .).

Two letters might be added: *E* for Evaluation and *Y* for "Why?" That makes it GOSSEY. Evaluation suggests the need for some overall assessment of the situation: "Is there a lesson to be learned from the city hall controversy?" This is another way of seeking meaning beyond the facts. The final *Y* merely suggests that the interviewer must not lose track of his shortest and most important question: "Why?"

The GOSS pattern, like any attempt to reduce human relations to simple formulas, is fraught with peril. It can be a crutch for lazy journalists who refuse to do their homework. Its value, however, is in reminding journalists that the history of mankind is that of forever reaching for goals—for good or for evil. Goals and the accompanying rewards are why people strive to climb mountains, write books, compose symphonies, build highways, explore space, work to make the world better— or work to exploit it for personal gain.

Some goals remain forever beyond one's grasp. But such is the material out of which dramatic nonfiction is fashioned.

PROBES

The probe is designed to encourage the respondent to explain or elaborate on something he's already said. You're writing a feature story about Professor Jones. A student tells you, "I feel uneasy whenever I step into his classroom." Do you merely quote that remark? Or do you ask probe questions in search of reasons? The latter course may provide significant insight into the character of the professor.

A counseling psychologist has developed an effective way of probing for detail. He simply picks a key word or two in the respondent's statement and repeats it softly in a gently questioning tone of voice.

"Feel uneasy . . ."

Then he waits for elaboration, which he seldom fails to get.

Other responses: "Really? . . . Why so? . . . Is it the teacher or the students or the room or what? . . . Tell me what you were thinking the last time you stepped into his room. . . ."

Eight Categories of Probes

Various scholars have placed probes into categories, such as the following set of eight. They are hypothetical responses to the remark of the wealthy dowager princess: "I've had thirty-three lovers in twenty years." So startling a revelation requires some finesse in the probe-response, as we shall see.

Passive "Hmmm. . . I see. . . ." (Deadpan expression.)

Responsive "Really? . . . thirty-three lovers? . . . How interesting! . . . You seem to have led an interesting life. . . ." (Smile, nod, raised eyebrow, eye contact.)

Negatively responsive "What a fickle woman you are! . . ." (Frown, scowl, avoidance of eye contact.)

Developing "Tell me more . . . Are you bragging or complaining? . . . Why so many? . . . What things do you most appreciate in a lover? . . ."

Clarifying "That's one and a half a year on the average; do you have affairs in sequence or concurrently? . . . Do these men know about each other? . . ."

Diverging "And yet you claim to be in the forefront of the feminist movement. . . . Do you also know men merely as friends? . . ."

Changing "Okay, now tell me about your interest in Renoir paintings. . . ."

Involving "Hey, Baby, who y'got in mind for Number thirty-four?"

SOLICITING OF QUOTATIONS

The problem with quotations is not getting them, since anything uttered by an interview respondent is potentially quotable. The problem is two-fold. The first part is recognizing the role of the quotation in one's written work. The second is encouraging a respondent to speak more colorfully, more candidly, more humanly, less formally—in short to utter compact statements that reveal character traits, capture moments of drama, or suggest certain universal truths. Many inexperienced writers do not take full advantage of the quotable quote. Examine, for example, this handling of a fragment of a controversial meeting of a student council. Referring to one of the speakers at the meeting, the student wrote:

> She alluded to the fact that the People's Coalition was devoid of the feminine gender, and she chastised the chairman of the coalition for falsely claiming to represent the interests of all the people.

The student had had a verbatim transcript of the meeting at his desk as he wrote. What the woman actually said was:

> Harry, there isn't a single woman in your People's Coalition. You don't represent the people at all—you represent only male chauvinist people. Power to the people—hell!

How much simpler, more concrete, and more dramatic the story would have been if the writer had simply used the quote. It not only adds color but it's six words shorter. It had never occurred to the student to use it to bring personality to his story. A further problem is the novice writer's tendency to put almost *everything* in quotes, including routine data. That way nothing stands out, and the special power of the quote is lost. A quote should be special, like a dash of spice, rather than routine. Thus in interviewing, the essence of soliciting quotations is simply knowing one when you hear it. You must listen with a special ear attuned to touches of color or idiosyncratic speech or especially succinct remarks. Without that ear, quotes have a way of whizzing by, never to be recaptured. Here are some typical ways quotes can be used in written work:

Human or Character-revealing

A wrangler leading tourists on mules down the steep trail to the bottom of the Grand Canyon: "Be mighty careful, ladies; I can always get plenty of tourists but a trained mule is hard to replace."

Humor, Homely Aphorisms

An Oregon cattle rancher: "There's three good ways to lose money: playing around with women is the nicest, playing the horses is the fastest, but the surest—the *surest* way to lose money is to be a cattle rancher."

Irony

Southern Ku Klux Klansman: "Before we start giving those niggers jobs, they've got to start improving their status quo."

Jargon

Former depression-era hobo: "Well, there we were, a couple of bindle stiffs just off the red ball express, diming up on the Main Stem."

Authentication

A World War II article suggested that correspondent Ernie Pyle was a shy, sensitive man. A quote from him authenticates the point:"I suffer agony in anticipation of meeting somebody for fear they won't like me."

Figures of Speech

"As a scholar, Professor Jones glosses over his subject like a hungry kingfisher gliding over the water and diving for whatever glitters."

Authority

The quote could be anything; what counts is who said it. The statement, "Our foreign policy is in a parlous state," means nothing if said by your average streetcar patron but has international implications if said by the secretary of state.

Once you know what you're looking for, soliciting quotations becomes relatively simple. When you hear one you like, you pounce on it. You savor it. You congratulate your respondent. Glowing from such praise, he will try hard to earn further plaudits. Sometimes you must prime the pump by coloring your own remarks and questions in largely the same manner that you hope the answers will sound like. Example:

> Q. Commissioner, a man in your precarious position, getting criticism from all sides, must feel lonely, like a man sitting on an iceberg in a storm-tossed sea.
>
> A. The hell you say! I think it's more like sitting on a keg of Oklahoma crude smoking a lighted cigar!

The journalist must take care, of course, in evaluating the answers to such "colored" questions. Had the commissioner agreed that his situation was akin to sitting on an iceberg, the quote should not have been used. It was yours, not his. You're seeking *original* thinking, not regurgitated primer questions.

Similarly, a recent statement attributed to the publisher of a sensational national weekly—*"Don't be afraid . . . to put words in people's mouths"*—belongs back where it reportedly was found: in the trash can. But nothing should prevent you from coming to an interview armed with primer quotations, your own or borrowed. The world of Mark Twain, Will Rogers, La Rochefoucauld, Oscar Wilde, and countless others is yours for the price of a library visit. Soon you'll be asking questions like this:

> Q. Senator, the controversies surrounding you remind me of Oscar Wilde's quote in *Dorian Gray:* "There's only one thing worse than being talked about, and that's not being talked about." What do you think?

Even if the response doesn't match the legendary Wilde wit and profundity, you'll have stimulated animated discussion. Here are some other suggestions:

Argumentation

Acting as a devil's advocate, you simply take another point of view. To avoid personal confrontation and assert your own neutrality, attribute the argument to somebody else: "Senator, your opponents might disagree. . . ." Better yet, be specific: "Congressman Claghorn opposes your policy on three counts and says . . ." The better prepared you are, the more effectively you can play your role of provocateur. Be careful, though— you might win the argument and lose the interview.

Sharp Probes

You can challenge your respondent to say things more colorfully by relentless pursuit of a soggy statement: "Why do you say that? . . . Do you really mean it? . . . How does this square with your earlier and seemingly conflicting statement? . . ." One reporter has adopted a practice of always "turning the coin over" as a means of challenging every statement. If you say it's a nice day, he'll find some way to skewer it: "What about the farmers whose crops are withering in the drought?"

Silence

The respondent has made what he thinks is a strong argument, and all he gets in response is silence. His own resulting panic seems to provoke him into returning with an even stronger, more dramatic, or more succinct comment. One research study suggests that an interviewer can help by using utterances such as "mm-hmm," which can extend the duration of the response by 30 to 90 percent.

SOLICITING OF ANECDOTES

We come now to the biggest bugaboo of most interviewers: prospecting for anecdotes. An anecdote is a "storiette" depicting a true experience and containing a primitive sense of plot and characterization. In feature articles, as well as in ordinary conversation, it is usually used to illustrate a point. Here's an example:

A young man was interviewing me to seek my views on a father's relationships with his children. I remarked at one point that "There are too darned many women in the lives of young children; fathers should take a more active role."

He asked, "Can you think of any humorous incidents that illustrate that statement?"

My mind went blank. I realized then why so few people can respond to that method of seeking anecdotes. It forced me to run my mind over countless half-remembered incidents and select one as "humorous." It required me to be a storyteller, which I am not. I'd have to tell it unrehearsed with vaguely remembered details. And how humiliating it would be if the interviewer didn't laugh. In all, there was too much work and risk. I took the easy way out.

"No," I said, "nothing comes to mind."

After he left, I reflected on the time my son Doug, then six, and I flipped over in a rubber raft while running the rapids of the Willamette River. There was the mountain climb with Scott, then nine. And the camping trip with Barbara, then eight, in the drenching rainstorm. What's funny is that each event represented a hardship—with no women present—that the kids *loved,* or so they said in retrospect. But the interviewer might not have seen the humor. Perhaps he'd have enjoyed Barbara's childish remark to a houseguest: "My Dad's a writer," she said proudly; "he writes checks." But what's the point of that? Besides, the atmosphere wasn't quite right for such comments. I wasn't sure I could trust the interviewer to respond sympathetically.

Such is the paranoia of your typical respondent. It is the key reason why cold-bloodedly asking for anecdotes seldom works. So what do you do? Beyond making the interview an "ordinary conversation" (in which anecdotes have a better chance of survival), here are three suggestions.

Concentrate on Incidents

Some interviewers, especially magazine writers, place major emphasis on incidents. They come armed with clippings and notes from preliminary interviews with wives and colleagues. They're forever approaching questions like this: "Your wife tells me about the time you got lost with the kids in the mountains . . ." or "I have this clipping about how you and the kids were rescued off a sandbar—I'd like to hear your version of the story."

Swapping Stories

Here's an example of a story told by an interviewer: "I can certainly see what you mean when you say kids are tougher and more self-reliant than most people think. My neighbor has this six-year-old boy who got lost the other day at the county fair. The parents were frantic. So what did the kid do? He walked home, all by himself. Four miles! Now *that's* self-reliant." Such a story primes the pump for the kind of anecdotes you'd like to get in return. It stimulates thinking along anecdotal lines. It gives a concrete example of the kind of experiences the interviewer considers noteworthy. You need not be a good storyteller. Quite the opposite. If you are especially good your respondent will be intimidated. But if you pick a soggy story and tell it badly, he'll easily top it with a story of his own. Then you can begin an escalation process.

Playing Hunches and Following Leads

A good interviewer can smell out an anecdote like a tiger in search of dinner. That's because he knows that most people's attitudes and convictions are born of specific, concrete experiences. People know to avoid touching a hot stove not because of an abstract philosophical principle but because they were burned once. If your mailman says "I hate dogs!" you can bet he's had some bad experiences with them. The proverb, "The straw that broke the camel's back," represents this truism. The interviewer therefore relentlessly sniffs out the incident that represents the last straw.* So an appropriate question for anecdote-soliciting might be, "This conviction you have about too many women in the lives of young children . . . I presume you've had some experiences that led you to that conclusion—would you tell me what happened?"

But don't expect to find anecdotes lying around waiting to be picked up like nuggets of gold. You have to process tons of raw conversational ore. Nowhere in interviewing is this more true than in prospecting for anecdotes. Many people are not natural storytellers (and it's wise to check the veracity of those who are). Anecdotes seldom emerge ready-made in an interview. Often you must pursue leads and hunches with gentle persistence. You must seek details—the grubby little items that will help bring an anecdotal scene alive when you put it down on paper: "What happened next? . . . What did she say? . . . What did you say? . . . What time was it? . . . What was the color of the room? . . . What was the weather? . . . Who else was there? . . ."

Here is a hypothetical interview that shows the gentle persistence required to draw people out. You are writing a feature story about Henry Harrison, a writer on your paper who has just won a national award for investigative reporting.

Q. Mr. Harrison, you've interviewed thousands of people—have you ever had a bad interview?

A. Oh, sure. Lots of people won't talk—

Q. I had in mind one that *you* muffed.

A. I'm sure I must have. Obviously some interviews go better than others. You're better prepared for some, or you feel better, and some people are easier to talk with than others.

Q. Are some kinds of people *invariably* hard for you to talk with?

A. Well, yeah.

Q. What kinds?

---

* Only slightly tongue in cheek, I offer "Metzler's Law": *The stronger the conviction held, the more dramatic the instances that shaped it are likely to be.*

A. I hate to say it, but I'm the world's worst guy at interviewing movie actresses and beauty queens—any kind of super-beautiful woman.

Q. Really? I should think that would be very easy and pleasant.

A. Oh, no—give me a good gangster any day.

Q. I suppose you've had some bad experiences interviewing women?

A. Quite a few.

Q. Such as?

A. Well, I muffed it with Marilyn, muffed it with Fonda, muffed it with Raquel—

Q. *All* of those?

A. And more—there was Yvonne and Sandra and—

Q. Which was the worst of those experiences?

A. Raquel without a doubt.

Q. Why?

A. I dunno. Don't ask. I just couldn't think of anything to say.

Q. Your mind went blank?

A. Yup.

Q. Tell me about it.

A. Hell, there's nothing to tell. My mind went blank, that's all.

Q. Is your mind still blank? I mean so far as recalling the incident?

A. Oh, I remember it vividly.

Q. Okay, then you actually did meet Raquel on one occasion?

A. Yup.

Q. What did you say to her?

A. That was the problem; I didn't say anything.

Q. All right, where was she when you met her?

A. On the movie set. It was between scenes. She was sitting by herself under a maple tree, and her press agent walks over and introduces us. Then he takes off and we're alone.

Q. Just you and Raquel?

A. Yeah. She says, "Hi. What was it you wanted to ask me?"

Q. And you said—

A. I stammered and grunted, that's all. My mind went blank.

Q. Then what happened?

A. She says, kind of laughing, "I suppose you'd like to know what I think about women's lib. That's the usual starting question these days." Well, that floored me.

Q. Why so?

A. Because it came back to me then—that *was* what I'd planned to ask. I figure this woman sees right through me. Well, I beat a hasty exit.

Q. How did you explain your sudden departure to Raquel?

A. I said, "Look, Sweetheart, I'm sorry but you'll have to excuse me. I've got this big shot gangster waiting for me over at the Plaza."

It may seem a hopelessly laborious way to get an anecdote. But that's precisely the way many anecdotes are obtained: tons of ore for an ounce of gold. This is what the raw ore would probably process down to:

> Prize-winning reporter Henry Harrison admits to one great failure as an interviewer. He's the world's worst guy at interviewing beautiful women.
>
> Sent to interview Raquel Welch one day, he pondered his first question and settled on women's lib. When they were alone, she said, "Hi. What was it you wanted to ask me?" His mind went blank. "I suppose you'd like to know what I think about women's lib," she prompted amiably.
>
> Stunned, Harrison thought to himself, "She sees through me."
>
> "Look, Sweetheart," he said, getting up to leave, "you'll have to excuse me. I've got this big shot gangster waiting for me at the Plaza."

CREATIVE QUESTIONS

The "creative" question is essentially an on-the-spot hypothesis to be tried out on the respondent for confirmation or denial. It is a plausible explanation for various things written or said about the subject at hand, including what's been said thus far in the interview. Some reporters have a knack for it. Their minds work creatively, sifting through all the conversational minutiae for bits and pieces that seem to add up in new and possibly novel ways. Some of these bits and pieces are not even verbal.

Why, for example, does the senator avoid your eyes whenever you ask him about economic recession? He said a moment ago that he agrees with the policy of selling wheat to Russia. But when you asked his evaluation of the success of detente, he evaded the question. He got to talking about the secretary of state and then rambled on about the Middle East. And last week a newspaper quoted him as saying, "I have more questions than answers about American foreign policy." Now how does *that* fit in?

As these and other items accumulate in your mind they may form a pattern, a possible meaning. You formulate a hypothesis—a possible explanation—and drop it into the conversation at the first opportunity.

Q. Senator, several things you've said today suggest that you may be considering a sharp departure from your previously announced support of detente. Have you in fact changed your thinking?

A. Good heavens! How did you reach *that* conclusion? [A typical reaction.]

Q. Just things you said.
A. Well, you're right! How perceptive! Yes, it's true. I feel I can
   no longer support the president's policy . . . etc.

If the hypothesis is denied, you've lost nothing. Perhaps you will have
gained some other explanation for the pieces that puzzle you. But when
such a hypothesis is confirmed, the interview often spirals upward with
renewed dynamic energy. That's because the senator is looking at you
in a new light, seeing you for the brilliant and perceptive observer that
you are (about time!).

FIVE

Interviewing Strategy

Q. General, how long have you been in military life?

A. If you don't know anything about me, why do you want to interview me?

The whole story of interviewing, suggests Richard Meryman, "is homework." Meryman specialized in personality portraits of such celebrities as Elizabeth Taylor and Hubert Humphrey for *Life*.

"I keep telling myself that the perfect interview is a perfect set of questions. The older I get, the more time I spend in advance on that list." Meryman does preliminary interviews with people close to his subject, asking and asking questions until "I start hearing things twice." In addition he reads whatever is already available on the subject, "all the time writing down questions and working out their phrasing." This groundwork averages out to about five hours for every one hour actually spent interviewing the subject.

A few days before meeting with his subject, Meryman becomes absorbed with his condition, in the manner of boxers and decathlon champions. "I don't touch any alcohol at all for about three days before an interview. I try to get a great deal of sleep. I don't eat starch or sugar. I spend the whole day or at least half the day before in bed. I eat steak for breakfast. Basically, I'm clearing my mind, getting my reflexes and attention as high as I can get them," because, as Meryman explains, "the important thing in an interview is not the first answer to a question on a particular topic. That answer should give you the clue to a second question on the subject, and that will lead to a third—and so on until you get to the nub. That's why I train, so that as the person is talking I am super-sensitive to those half-articulated hints which clue me into follow-up questions."

Meryman is convinced that "There is always about a person a single, central question. All this preparation is to try and figure out what that is. If you get the question, and the answer, you've got the key." [1]

Perhaps not all journalists can afford the luxury of spending the day before an interview in bed. But don't lose sight of the point: interviewing strategy must begin with preparation. Interviewers might, in fact, benefit from the advice philosopher William James once offered to teachers: know your subject thoroughly and then trust to luck. An interviewer who knows his subject can move down any one of numerous conversational paths with his respondent. He can detect fine nuances and half-expressed ideas that, when explored more fully in the conversation, produce fresh ideas and insights. And because he has read widely about the subject, he can separate the new and refreshing from the old and hackneyed.

The term *strategy,* as used here, should not necessarily imply an adversary relationship. It simply means planning ahead so that you'll know how to approach your respondent and ease comfortably into the topics about which you intend to inquire. A famous interviewer of World War I compared it to "salesmanship." Isaac F. Marcosson, who interviewed such figures as Theodore Roosevelt and General John J. Pershing, said that he invariably made it a point to find out all he could about a man before going to see him. "This is precisely what any good salesman will do."

All great men have an interest, such as yachting, art, great books, "and with that interest you can disarm prejudice and even sterilize opposition to your purpose," Marcosson wrote in his 1919 book, *Adventures in Interviewing.* He added that each interview must be pitched on a "separate and distinct plane. Some silent men must be swept irresistibly into conversation on the high tide of talk. You take the initiative. Then too there is the type who begins to speak the moment you see him. All you have to do is to guide the current of words."

Successful interviewers also speak of "pushing the right button" to stimulate a current of words. This too involves knowing your subject, for it is the prepared interviewer who most often finds "luck" on his side. *New Yorker* writer A. J. Liebling opened an interview with jockey Eddie Arcaro with the question, "How many holes longer do you keep your left stirrup than your right?" That started Arcaro talking enthusiastically for an hour with virtually no further comments from Liebling. "I can see you've been around riders a lot," Arcaro said. Liebling had, but only

[1] Editors' Note, *Life* Magazine, July 7, 1972. © 1972 Time, Inc. Reprinted by permission.

during the week before the interview. He had learned through homework that jockeys ride longer on their left side on American tracks (*The Most of A. J. Liebling*).

Such "luck" comes easily to the prepared interviewer.

PLANNING AN INTERVIEW: A HYPOTHETICAL EXAMPLE

Suppose now that you are a staff writer for a magazine, let's say a city magazine like *Philadelphia* or *Washingtonian,* or maybe a newspaper magazine supplement. The point of the magazine context is simply to assume that your proposed interview is more leisurely and comprehensive than a tight-to-the-deadline news report. We'll say you're planning to interview the police chief in your city. Seven steps are basic in the pre-interview preparation.

1. Definition of your purpose
2. Preinterview research
3. Character assessment of respondent
4. Specific questions or "areas of inquiry"
5. Anticipated answers
6. Request for an interview
7. The "game plan"

1. Your Purpose

You could have a hundred reasons for interviewing the police chief, and each would dictate a different strategy. Your magazine is doing a story on rape and you want the chief's views on the problem. The city has quietly put about a dozen female officers into patrol cars and you want the chief's assessment of the successes and failures of this program. You're doing a piece on organized crime or increasing violence or white collar crime or special police "SWAT" units ("Special Weapons and Tactics")— and in all of these possible stories you need the insights and perceptions of the city's chief law enforcement officer. Or you've uncovered, after long investigation, evidence of corruption within the department. That interview would certainly call for different strategy than the others. (The corruption interview might not be so difficult as you think. You don't go to the chief for an interview until you have firm, hard-to-refute evidence that will stand up in court. When you do, you gently confront the chief to ask for his reactions, refutations, and/or promises of reform. Angry words need not be exchanged. With the proper evidence in hand, you can afford to be especially gentle and considerate, though persistent. Only a hopelessly insecure interviewer would attempt to browbeat a respondent in these circumstances.)

Specific purposes are easier to pursue through interviews than vague purposes. So are purposes that both interviewer and respondent agree are worthy of public discussion. Both parties should have a clear understanding of the purpose. It should serve them as a guiding beacon, lighting the way for the interview along a well-defined pathway and away from meaningless and time-consuming diversions.

Let's say, then, that you are writing a major article about policewomen. The city, with much pressure from the federal government, has quietly relaxed its barriers against hiring women for police patrol jobs. Women are on regular patrol duty on the same basis as men. Now, with a dozen women on the job, you are preparing an article on their effectiveness and on their experiences as pioneers attempting to settle in this traditional male stronghold, the City Police Department.

The chief will be among your first interviews. Why first? Shouldn't he be among the last interviews, after you've gathered information from lower levels? Perhaps. Definitely so in the case of the "confrontation" described above. But experience tells you that in most "in-house" interviewing (i.e., interviewing many persons within an organization), you go to the leaders, titular and/or de facto, first. Police departments, especially, tend to be rigid and semimilitary bureaucracies whose members are rightfully suspicious of the press; any experienced cop can tell you about the times he's been "burned" by arrogant or incompetent reporters. If you are to deal with the subject of policewomen candidly and honestly, then you must create an interviewing climate in which candor and honesty can thrive. You start by *being* open and honest yourself. You then get the right people interested. These people will pass the word along: you can be trusted. They have found you not only honest and sincere, but challenging and stimulating: you know what you are talking about. You've done your homework. That gets around, too.

Even if it doesn't, starting at the top has benefits. To say to a skeptical respondent, "Yes, I've already talked with the chief," tends to relax people. That the chief is not loved in all quarters seems to make little difference. He remains the head of the department, a powerful figure. His willingness to answer your questions gives tacit approval to your work—thus strong credentials that can open many doors.

The chief, then, will be perhaps the third of the twenty to thirty interviews you may do for this article. The first two may be preliminary discussions with the department's public relations officer and with a knowledgeable "outsider," such as a newspaper police reporter or an interested member of the city council. The chief might also be the *last* interview if you find you need to talk with him again after you've interviewed others. Nobody said you can't try for *two* interviews.

What, then, is the purpose of your first interview? *The chief's preliminary evaluation of the experiences, accomplishments, and problems of the dozen pioneering women serving as police patrol officers.* That will do for a start. You can redefine it more specifically, if necessary, as you move along the remaining steps of preinterview planning.

2. Preinterview Research

Informal grassroots observation is among the best kinds of preliminary research. Through it you learn what people are talking about. When friends greet you on the street—"Hi, whatcha been up to lately?"—you tell them you're working on a magazine piece on policewomen. That's a coincidence, they say. Just the other day they (or their spouses or friends) had an encounter with a policewoman, they tell you—and they proceed to provide the details. Or at a social gathering you quietly let word get around about your project. Surprisingly soon the room comes alive with talk about female cops. You begin to pick up snippets of conversation.

Where do they carry their guns? . . . Not in their purses, I hope; can you imagine searching through your purse for a gun like my sister searches for her car keys? . . . I understand they ride around in squad cars with men partners—wouldn't the guys' wives object? . . . I read a piece in the paper about how some gal flipped a 250-pound drunk over her shoulder and put the cuffs on him. . . . I think women would make better detectives than men. . . . Can they stomach the sordid views of life that cops get? . . . A rape victim would probably prefer to talk with a woman cop. . . .

You carefully monitor such conversations—including the misinformation and the male chauvinist prejudice—for their basic value: they represent what interests people. That's a good starting point for planning your interviews.

Library research is the second preliminary step. A former magazine editor suggests that a writer may skim two dozen books and perhaps a hundred articles, reports, memoranda, and other documents in the writing of one five thousand-word article. It is this kind of research that makes the difference between a seventy-five dollar article and a fifteen hundred dollar article—between a superficial Sunday feature and a comprehensive magazine piece (Rose, 1967).

A newspaper library, if you have access to one, is a good starting point. News clippings announcing the first woman to join the police force will probably be there, along with clips of any controversy or litigation involved. So will clips on the chief himself: interviews, features, the original announcements of his appointment as chief. You may also learn of local problems: organized crime, prostitution, conflicts with college rebels, low morale among officers, threats of labor strikes. You note with interest, for example, the clipping that describes a group of feminists invading the chief's office to present him a trophy: "Male Chauvinist Pig of the Year."

The city library is another important stop. In the reference section, you find reference books and indexes that contain leads to valuable information. Here are some of the primary ones:

New York Times Index gives brief abstracts of significant stories. Under the listing Police (general), for example, you learn of a Police Foundation study in 1974 that finds no significant difference in the performance of male and female police officers on patrol duty in Washington, D. C. This was based on a comparison of eighty-six male and eighty-six female recruits.

Reader's Guide to Periodical Literature lists atricles for general magazines. By consulting listings under Crime, Law Enforcement, and Policewomen over the past half-dozen years, you find many articles of interest, ranging from "Women Make Good Cops" *(New York Times Magazine)* to "Policewomen: How Well Are They Doing a Man's Job?" *(Ladies' Home Journal)*. By securing back copies of these and other magazines, you learn more about the role of women. You learn that in 1974 New York had 733 women officers, Washington 260, Peoria, Illinois 11. You find that the 1973 Crime Control Act forbids sex discrimination by police departments receiving federal funds. One major issue centers on physical minimums: the typical police minimums, 5′ 7″ height and 140 weight, bar 97 percent of the nation's women from becoming officers.

Your research will go beyond policewomen, of course. To talk a police chief's language, you need a broader view. You learn from general articles that crime and violence are up, that citizens in some cities are forming neighborhood watch groups for burglary protection, that more women are involved in crime and violence than ever before, that police departments are increasingly concerned with public image and community relations.

The library has other useful indexes. To list a few:

Business Periodical Index

Education Index

Women's Studies Abstracts

Public Affairs Information Service Bulletin (PAIS)

Playboy Index

Social Sciences Index

Humanities Index

Biography Index

Book Review Digest
Wall Street Journal Index
Index to U.S. Government Periodicals
The Times Index (The Times of London)
Cumulative Book Index
Christian Science Monitor Index

Another step is your library's own card catalog file, which lists books that are actually in the library. Perhaps you check out a few of these: Peter Horne's *Women in Law Enforcement* for a general view, or Dorothy Uhnak's *Policewoman* for a graphic, personal view (such as learning in an orientation lecture that a cop eventually finds nothing unusual in examining a butchered corpse and then eating a hefty lunch an hour later).

You may also look for general books on police work (*Issues in Police Administration* seems a likely title) as a means of learning about the concerns of a police chief, so you can talk his language. Two reports by the Police Foundation catch your eye, *Women in Policing* and *Policewomen on Patrol: Final Report*. You check these out of the library; the latter report turns out to be the basis of most of the newspaper and magazine articles you've read since 1974.

All of these are mere snippets of the vast amounts of research materials available in even a modest-sized library. The reference books cited here are by no means a complete list. Every serious interviewer should have a copy of Barton and Bell's *Reference Books: A Brief Guide* or a similar listing of reference works.

3. Character Assessment

The more you know about the chief, the more you can adapt your style of interviewing to his personality. Is he quiet or talkative? Is he open and candid or suspicious and cunning? Will you have to take the conversational initiative or merely sit back and direct the torrent of words?

You learn, we'll say, that he's sensitive and a little shy. He keeps a low profile, leaving most press interviews to his deputies. He smokes a pipe, wears civilian clothes, enjoys reading books about travel, adventure, and the outdoors. He's considered by his colleagues to be a "homespun philosopher." He's written three articles for police journals, and you get copies of them from the police public relations office, along with other reports and routine public documents. The articles deal with (1) a none-too-successful attempt to establish neighborhood watch programs to prevent burglary, (2) a successful antishoplifting campaign, and (3) a plea for moderation of the hardline approach to college rebels. The chief is said to be wary of seeing women on police patrol, exposed to danger for which he feels they are less equipped than men. But he acknowledges that he doesn't have much choice in the light of federal regulations. And what do you do with this information? It will help you find ways to talk with the chief on a person-to-person basis, thus enhancing rapport. You might even consider carrying matches to help him light his pipe if, like many pipe smokers, he expends them at an astonishing rate.

Where do you get such information? It comes surprisingly easily from friends and colleagues of the chief, from secretaries, from members of the family.

4. Specific Questions or Areas of Inquiry

Should your questions be written down? How precisely should they be phrased? Beginning journalists tend to write down their questions precisely as they plan to ask them. As they gain experience they tend to rely more on on-the-spot improvisations. One problem with the perfectly phrased question is that it never seems to fit the context of the conversation. You inhibit freewheeling discussion when you read off a question that's out of context. That's why many interviewers prefer to jot down key-word notes on the areas to be covered:

> general observations on women officers
>
> views on women exposed to danger
>
> how they shoot, cope with violence, handle domestic disputes, etc.
>
> differences in the way they work, if any, compared to men
>
> chief's views of 1974 Police Foundation report
>
> changes necessary to adapt to presence of women in dept.
>
> physical minimums problem (5' 7", 140 lbs too severe?)
>
> identify strengths and weaknesses of females as cops
>
> male attitudes in dept.—chauvinism, hostility, etc.
>
> chief's own attitude toward women
>
> what about "pig of year" award?

This partial list excludes "icebreaker" topics designed to get the interview off to a friendly, informal start. The list is arranged from the most innocuous (starting here with a request for predictable platitudes) to the most threatening ("pig of year" award). Whether on paper or in your mind, you ultimately end up with questions, of course. Here are some approaches to questions.

You can ask them in a pristinely neutral tone: "Chief Brown, do you feel that any changes are necessary in the police department's policy and procedures to accommodate women as officers?"

Or directly (i.e., with more urgency): "What changes must the department make to accommodate women as officers?"

Or obliquely: "Recently the Police Foundation issued a report suggesting that departments must make certain changes to prepare for women as officers. . . . How do you feel about that?"

Or a "funnel" series that starts with a broad question and narrows it down to specifics: "Has the presence of women brought any changes in the department? . . . What kinds of changes? . . . What about policy changes? . . . What about the policy on height and weight minimums? . . ." (A "no" answer to the first would not necessarily preclude the others, especially after you've cited some evidence from the Police Foundation study.)

Sometimes a "filter" question must be asked: "Chief, what was your overall impression of the 1974 Police Foundation study on policewomen?" (You ask it that way rather than "Have you read the study?" to avoid embarrassing him. If he hasn't read it, he'll say so or you'll sense it soon enough from his bumbling, evasive answer.)

Generally you should avoid "leading" questions, ones that suggest the expected answer: "You *do* believe that women are a splendid asset to the police department, don't you?"

Also avoid personally confronting kinds of questions and comment: "Chief, you're dead wrong; there is absolutely no difference between men and women!" That engenders personal antagonisms that damage candid response. If you want to bring up an opposing point of view, attribute it to someone else and be a little more tactful: "Chief, the Police Foundation study suggests that women perform just as well as men on patrol in Washington, D. C. . . ."

And *certainly* the interviewer should avoid "loaded" questions: "Chief, considering the outrageously hostile attitudes of yourself and your male officers, and considering the awesome ineptitude of the police force generally, don't you think it's only poetic justice that you should be cited as Male Chauvinist Pig of the Year?"

5. Preparing for Anticipated Answers

You don't have to wait for an answer before you can plan a follow-up question. If you ask, "Chief, are you concerned about the performance of women officers in barroom brawls and similar situations?" you'll know what to ask next no matter what his answer. If he says yes, you'll ask "Why?" or "Have there been incidents that tend to confirm your concern?" If he says no, you'll ask whether they have actually been tested in such frays and, if so, with what result?

6. Planning Your Initial Request for an Interview

The best advice here is start with a common denominator, preferably as seductive a one as you can find. As you reflect on your preliminary research, an obvious one suggests itself in this case: the chief's published articles. There is probably not a person alive who writes—whether professionally or as a sideline—who can resist the approach, "I read your article on _____." To that you add a transition to the topic you want to discuss: "One of the things that interested me when I read your piece on softening the hardline approach with college kids is the question of women as police officers. I'm curious to know if you think they would tend to be more agreeable with your point of view than men. . . ."

What you frequently get in response is an attempt to answer the question on the spot. That would be the time to mention that you're doing an article on just such a topic and that you're eager to have the chief's views on the subject. You may, of course, have to go through channels—through a deputy, or the community relations department, or even via letter. Be patient.

7. The "Game Plan"

Your opening plays along with your whole strategy can now be firmed up for the interview itself. You'll plan to break the ice with talk of mutual interests: writing, books, travel, the out-of-doors. You will move, slowly or swiftly depending on circumstances, into a full explanation of your purpose and your plans to do an honest, fair-minded assessment of the topic. You might then go back to the original question posed on the phone (women's views on confrontations with college kids), a topic he may have thought about in the meantime.

Can a standard format be cited for the sequence in which you ask questions? Beyond the obvious points—start on a pleasantly innocuous note and work gradually toward the "bombs"—I think not, not if this is to be a freewheeling discussion in which candor can reign. You are not, after all, asking for favored detergents. You are asking about people, about human feelings, about the "real" plight of the female cop. The problem with the rigid schedule of questions—the kind used for opinion survey interviewing—is that the answer to Question Number One may include partial answers to numbers three and five. Do you insist on going back to number two next? You may dampen the conversation. On the other hand, by finishing three and five, you enliven discussion but emerge with disorganized notes. Which do you prefer—a lively, candid conversation or organized notes?

One workable format (perhaps "attitude" would more precisely describe it) is the rambling dictates of natural curiosity. This means letting the conversation flow naturally and with minimal guidance. So long as your "areas of inquiry" are being covered, you ask the questions more or less as they occur to you. "You start a question and it's like starting a stone," said Robert Louis Stevenson. "You sit quietly on the top of a hill and away the stone goes, starting others." (From *The Strange Case of Dr. Jekyll and Mr. Hyde.*)

Chronology is another natural pattern for ordering your questions and guiding the conversation. You start at the beginning of any situation and work your way through the present and into the future. This concept can be broken down into six basic questions. *How did it begin (or how did you first get involved)? . . . What's happened since then? . . . What is the situation at present? . . . What will (may) happen next? . . . What will (should) you do about it? . . . Is there some basic lesson that others can learn from this experience?*

In the policewomen example, you could ask the chief to tell you his (or the department's) first experience with female cops and then let him take you through the sequence of events since then. Both you and he can use chronology as the basic pattern for the flow of information. Whatever the pattern, the interviewer must learn to use "foundation questions" that insure his understanding of a situation before he can proceed. No matter how well prepared he is, the interviewer invariably comes upon matters he's not heard of before: new situations, incidents, procedures, alliances. If he is to write about them, he must understand them. Take this interview snippet as an example:

Q. Chief, can you cite specific areas of police work in which women have proved especially effective?

A. Yes, one in particular stands out: our use of women officers in the high crime task force.

High crime task force? The interviewer had not heard of it, despite preparation. Should he pretend that he already knows about it? Should he nod knowingly and hope that the chief will drop some clue that will lead to his understanding? An appalling number of neophytes will do precisely that, so self-conscious are they about their own inadequacies. An interviewer better prepared for the "unpredictable" will relax and ask the necessary background questions.

Q. High crime task force? Sounds interesting. What is it?

A. It's a modified version of team policing. We get computer print-outs on crime statistics that tell us when and where crime is likely to be at its worst. We know, for example, that Sunday nights are bad for burglary down in the warehouse district of town. So we send in this special task force operating independently under the command of a sergeant. We find that just the presence of marked cars reduces crime in some areas by as much as 50 percent whether we make any arrests or not.

Q. I see. How many cars are involved?

A. It varies. Usually about eight.

Q. What happens to the potential burglars during this time?

A. Often they get desperate. They like to operate in familiar surroundings. When we flood an area with the task force for just one night, the crime continues to be low for a week or more. What frequently happens is that these burglars are forced into operating in areas they're not familiar with. They make more mistakes and therefore get caught more often. . . .

Slowly and precisely the interviewer builds his own understanding of the task force concept. Once he's satisfied that he knows what it is, he can return to the original purpose of the discussion: the role of female officers.

VARY YOUR STRATEGY

In the end, interviewing strategy involves two considerations.

1. The interviewer should have full knowledge of his subject. The more you know the more you can relax and immerse yourself in the conversation and all its nuances.

2. The interviewer must develop a unique strategy for each respondent. The low-key approach may work for the sensitive police chief who doesn't like reporters. What if your respondent is known to fire back answers like a machine gun, seldom permitting a second question to be asked? President Theodore Roosevelt had just such a reputation. Lincoln Steffens, a famous contemporary journalist, once interviewed the president as he was being shaved by his barber. Steffens contrived to have the barber tarry at shaving the lower lip. This quieted the squirming, irrepressible Teddy Roosevelt long enough to allow Steffens to interject a complex question. (From *The Autobiography of Lincoln Steffens.*)

Whatever your strategy, you must face the likelihood that the conversation will not go as planned. People are unpredictable, often delightfully so. A chance remark—"some people think women make especially good detectives because of their precise ways"—may cause the police chief to say something that will change the entire picture. Perhaps he tells you he's planning a major reorganization with appointment of a female chief of detectives. You're the first outsider to know. This may change your interviewing objectives. It may call for a new strategy. You'll be better prepared for the changes and better able to improvise new questions because of the thoroughness of your original planning. Perhaps it was your thoroughness that prompted the chance remark that got the interview off on its new tack. And now you have something totally unexpected to write about. Count your blessings, and make that lady chief of detectives your next interview.

SIX

Multiple-Interview Projects

Q. Dr. Eisenbach, in the thirty seconds remaining, would you please summarize
your views on the meaning of man's existence?

A. May I respectfully suggest that your
viewers would be better served by thirty
seconds of silence? . . .

Many, perhaps most, journalistic articles are based on a variety of research
materials, including several interviews rather than just one. The writer
conducting several interviews encounters some new situations unknown to
the single-interview approach.

For one, what one person tells you another will contradict. Interview
five witnesses to a train wreck and you will get five different versions.
Witnesses to a 1959 air crash in Maryland said they saw the plane explode
at thirteen hundred feet altitude, at nine thousand feet, and at various
levels in between. They said the explosion came first, then the plane
disintegrated in midair. They said the plane began to break apart in
midair, then it exploded. In short, they agreed on almost nothing.

You'll also find that people talk about you. Word soon gets around
about your project. If your first interviews are successful from the respondents' point of view (i.e., you can be trusted, you ask perceptive questions,
you listen carefully, you're sympathetic), then word moves on ahead of
you, and your subsequent interviews become ever more productive. The
opposite is also true; people clam up if they hear bad things about you.
This is particularly true when you're interviewing in small communities
or organizations, such as a small town, a police department, an industrial
plant, a legislature, city hall, and so on.

In multiple interviewing you will find, too, that what one respondent considers a deep secret another will freely tell you. Some may even seek you out to tell you what they know of the topic at hand—and to make sure their points of view get a hearing.

Finally, you have the problem of sorting through all the often-conflicting material and trying to figure out what it means. You have more material than you can possibly use; how do you decide what to include and what to exclude?

The answer is that you will be "writing" your article, at least in your head, even as you are conducting the interviews. Indeed, your interviewing style is inextricably linked to your writing style. And writing styles have changed dramatically through the decade of the 1970s. Something called "new journalism" has brought more attention to dramatization through the techniques of the fiction writer: narrative, description, characterization, dialogue, scenes, even a sense of plot.

This has serious implications for the interviewer. What the fiction writer can dream up out of his head the nonfiction writer must try to duplicate. He does so not by faking scenes and dialogue but by intense interviewing and concentrated observation. Often the interviewer-observer is present when revealing scenes take place. Or the scenes may be duplicated by interviewing that places great emphasis on details and step-by-step narrative: "What happened next? . . . What did she say? . . . What was your reply? . . . What were you thinking to yourself at the time? . . ."

The growth of dramatic techniques for factual writing is by no means limited to books and magazines. Newspaper feature writers are using them increasingly, as witness this opening in an article by Sally Quinn in the *Washington Post* (reprinted in Babb's *Writing in Style*):

> Christine Chubbuck flicked her long dark hair back away from her face, swallowed, twitched her lips only slightly and reached with her left hand to turn the next page of her script. Looking down on the anchor desk she began to read: "In keeping with Channel 40's policy of bringing you the latest in"—she looked up from the script, directly into the camera and smiled a tentative smile. Her voice took on a sarcastic tone as she emphasized "blood and guts . . . and in living color." She looked back down at her script, her left hand shook almost unnoticeably.

Quinn went on to describe, detail by chilling detail, the death by suicide of a twenty-nine-year-old Florida television personality who "in living color" proceeded to pick up a .38 caliber revolver, point it to the lower back of her head, and pull the trigger. The story went on to retrace the woman's life through postmortem interviews with colleagues and family.

Even "interior monologue," the literary device by which the fiction writer crawls into the mind of a character and shows him thinking things, can be duplicated by the nonfiction writer. To do so, you need to ask your subject what he *thought* in any given situation in addition to what he said and did. You can't always be sure of getting an honest answer, of course. (Nor can you be sure when asking what he said and did.) But if you know your character well enough through previous interviews and research, you can tell what *seems* in character. Interior monologue takes several written forms; here's one example.

> As he climbed the steep trail to Opie Dildock Pass, the old forest ranger's thoughts turned to bygone days. Twenty years ago, he thought to himself, the forest trails would be deserted this time of year. You'd have the whole wilderness to yourself. Now look at it. Young kids on the trail, housewives, college girls, even grandmothers. Women! Twenty years ago no self-respecting woman would venture into the mountains alone. Look at them in their college sweatshirts and patched dungarees. Would he ever get used to seeing young women on the trails?

Perhaps, as many argue, there is nothing new about the "new" journalism. Critics point to Daniel Defoe and Mark Twain as early new journalists, and perhaps they are right. What is new is the *increasing* use of such graphic narrative detail in nonfiction writing. The traditional inverted pyramid technique of the newswriter is not likely to be replaced soon, but newswriting styles are being freed to permit the use of narratives in certain kinds of news stories as, for example, a dramatic rescue of a child from the tenth floor of a burning building in an otherwise routine fire story.

All of this has a profound impact on the techniques of interviewing. Many newswriters are no longer content with the wham-bam "two phone calls and a quick three hundred words" type of story. So they employ more thorough methods of interviewing. They press for graphic details that will make even a routine news story sparkle with new vividness. And they interview a lot of different people.

THE NONFICTION ARTICLE DEFINED

Before you can start a multiple-interview project, you must know something about the anatomy of the nonfiction article so that you will know what kind of detail to seek through your interviews. You know, for example, that you need anecdotes. Description. Dialogue. Above all you need a central theme that ties together all these fragments. But you must not settle too quickly on the theme because, as Sherlock Holmes once remarked to Watson, it is a capital offense to theorize before the facts are in.

You will, of course, begin to form impressions. In the case of an article on women as police officers, you'll perhaps begin to sense that women are, indeed, equal to the task of policing. Or maybe you'll sense that methods of policing will change somewhat with women as officers. You'll begin to develop hypotheses that will help to direct your subsequent interview questions as you set about confirming or denying those hypotheses. The work of the interviewer in multi-interview projects thus becomes a continual process of seeing and defining—and then reseeing and redefining if subsequent interviews produce evidence suggesting that your first definitions are inadequate.

Perhaps ultimately you'll conclude from your research that "Women make good cops." Or you might conclude that "Women will make good cops if and when male chauvinistic attitudes change." With a theme in hand your next task is to find further specific documentation to support the theme: facts, figures, anecdotes, instances—concrete details that help show dramatically that "women make good cops" if that is your theme.

The nonfiction article, as described here, includes magazine articles, nonfiction books, comprehensive news reports and features (as differentiated from spot news reports). Such articles tend to be more thoughtful and substantive than the quick news reports because they are done with greater care and thought. And they take more time, both in interviewing and writing. They are actually an amalgamation of three basic types of writing; this should be kept in mind when contemplating which persons to interview and what kinds of information to seek through the interviews.

1. The Factual Report

The article deals with real people, real situations, and actual events, using facts that are provably true. Although interpretations may be debatable, the facts themselves are or should be irreproachable.

2. The Essay

The article expresses, unapologetically, a definite point of view or theme. These views tend to come in three categories: (1) passionate opinions ("Let's give women cops a chance!"), (2) interpretations of reality ("Women make good cops"), and (3) the posing of questions or issues ("Do women make good cops?"). The first is the strongest and most controversial, but the second is more typical of articles. As a writer you have explored an issue thoroughly and have emerged with what you believe to be an accurate interpretation of it: women make good cops. The third category is weakest; at best it is an airing of both sides of an issue. At worst it is a set of self-cancelling platitudes.

3. The Short Story

The factual realities and interpretations are dramatized through scenes, dialogue, character sketches, description, and sometimes even a well-defined plot. The concept boils down to an oft-repeated maxim of the nonfiction writer: *show, don't just tell.* People do this all the time in conversation. Let's say that you want to suggest that among the police-women, Jill, the farm girl from Nevada, has a rural, cornball sense of humor. The reader is cheated if you merely *say* it. So you *show* a typical cornball remark: "Out where I come from the jackrabbits are so big that a nearsighted rancher rounded up 567 of them before he discovered they weren't part of his cattle herd."

It is in this show-don't-tell arena that the skill of the interviewer becomes especially important. Facts you can get from reading. The same is true with philosophical concepts. Even the dullest of documents contain facts and concepts. Indeed, they are dull because that's *all* they contain. The magazine article, by contrast, contains life and drama and style by providing information obtainable only by personal observation and interviewing.

THE SEARCH FOR DRAMA AND COLOR

To produce in your writing touches of human color such as Jill's jack-rabbits remark, you must create the kind of interview atmosphere in which Jill feels free to be herself. Then she can talk about jackrabbits without fear of ridicule. She's most likely to do so in an atmosphere of friendly and amiable conversation. She's not likely to do it in the aloof, hostile atmosphere of a *Meet the Press* style of interview. So the closer your interview comes to "ordinary conversation," the more likely it is that human information—anecdotal experiences, colorful observations, off-guard remarks—will emerge.

The style and direction of your interviews are also dictated by other "literary devices" in your writing. You know, for example, that an intimate portrayal of one policewoman is vastly more interesting than a superficial glance at twelve. So you set out to find *the* personality that best fits your literary-journalistic requirement: a woman who is appealing, personable, human, progressive, but not extreme. Her "faults" are charming idiosyncracies: cornball humor, for instance. So you select one officer, Jill, for this role of central protagonist, and you interview her at length, from childhood on. You constantly watch for human touches, such as her childhood adulation of FBI agents whose pictures she used to cut from magazines.

But you need supporting interviews, just as you need an orchestra behind the guest soloist. These interviews may be less comprehensive and more pointed. You will interview Julie because she was the first female officer and you know this pioneering role is often the roughest and most dramatic. . . . Jane because you want her story of how she single-handedly subdued a bunch of barroom toughs. . . . Mary because you suspect her exceptional beauty may have brought experiences unlike those of the others. . . . Gayle because her militant feminism takes her in philosophical directions quite different from the others. . . . Helen because she is a brilliant intellectual whose goal is to earn a Ph.D. and write books on law enforcement theory . . . and so on.

The good writer knows, too, that one concrete incident is worth a thousand generalities. It's cheap and easy to quote women complaining about "chauvinistic attitudes" among the men, but more precious and dramatic to describe one clearcut and effective example of the problem.

The writer also knows which scenes to flash briefly and which to linger over. Some incidents involve action, mystery, intrigue, and suspense. Others are merely violent and coarse—lacking therefore in literary delicacy and effect. So you devote a mere line to the policewoman who got slugged in the eye by an irate motorist to whom she was giving a ticket. But you spend almost a page about the policewomen who entered a dingy house, gun drawn, in search of an armed and dangerous fugitive. You create tension in the reader by subtly alluding to the expectation of sudden death. Perhaps you show the woman thinking to herself as she moves silently from room to room in the semidarkened house. *If I got a bullet between the eyes, I'd never even hear the shot.*

And where do you get *that* information? By asking, of course.

The climax approaches. A shadowy figure, gun in hand, looms against the opposite wall. She tenses, her finger tight on the trigger of her own .38. She slowly raises the gun, and so does the figure. In less than a second she realizes the truth—the "figure" is her own reflection in a full-length mirror. *Thank God I didn't shoot.* Shooting would have required six reports of explanation, not to mention weeks of male chauvinistic ridicule from fellow officers.

The house was empty all along. But the writer doesn't say so. Literary striptease is more artistic and more effective than naked truth. Your purpose, after all, is not to say whether the house was empty. It is to show the cop in action so that the reader might relive some of the tension. The reader might thereby perceive that the expectation of violence is more unnerving than the reality of it. All of this you must keep in mind at the interviewing stage. You cannot fake it later.

Finally the skilled writer knows that among the best literary devices is factual detail, defined by *Newsweek's* Karl Flemming as "the tireless gathering of that seemingly unimportant minutiae that gives people and places vivid color and unique character."

Thus in interviewing the policewoman who entered the house in search of the armed fugitive, you press for details. The best way, usually, is to let her tell the story first in her own way. Then you go over it again for the missing details. What did the house look like? Was it occupied or abandoned, large, small, brick, wood, a tarpaper shack, or what? What kind of person was the fugitive? How old? Why was he wanted? Had he shot or harmed anyone in the past? What kind of weapon was he thought to be carrying? What was the weather outside? Hot, cold, muggy, balmy, raining, snowing? What time of day? Was the house lighted or dark? What kind of gun did the cop have? Did she draw it from a holster or purse or what? In what hand did she hold it? Had she ever drawn her gun before? Ever fired a shot at anyone? Was she noted for marksmanship, i.e., high scores in target practice? Was she alone or with other cops? Where were they at the time? What was she wearing—uniform, plain clothes, what? How did she move inside the house—stealthily, quickly, slowly? How did she enter doorways? How was the house furnished? Did she smell or hear anything while searching? What did she say to her fellow cops afterward?

Obviously you wouldn't use all this material in your story. Art, as practiced by the nonfiction writer, is largely selection of detail. But without a thorough briefing of the situation, how will you know which details to select?

NEW DIRECTIONS FOR PROJECT INTERVIEWING

To the journalist, all of the above adds up to the need for greater skills in interviewing, greater candor, greater attention to detail, and a lot more interviews. In his book, *Depth Reporting,* Neale Copple describes a writer who consulted nearly 350 sources for a story on the political beliefs of college students on one campus. He sent questionnaires to 300 students and interviewed 43 other students and professors.

Floyd Miller interviewed at least 100 persons in the small community of Nyack, New York, for a dramatic *Reader's Digest* account of a train-school bus collision that killed five teenagers and injured many more.

"What they tell you they have to tell of their own volition," he said (*Quill,* June 1974). "Your reputation must go ahead of you—your reputation as one who is sympathetic and who can receive information without judging."

The reputation is only one of several vital considerations that make the multiple-interview project distinctly different from an equal number of unrelated interviews. If reputations get around, so do rumors. A sociologist, interviewing homosexuals in one city, found that many respondents could not only identify previous respondents but they could repeat almost verbatim what had been discussed (Lenznoff, 1956).

Here are some other important considerations.

Key People

You must identify people whose good will is important to your work. Whether they are de facto leaders or merely persons of great influence, you must work with them to defuse hostility and aid your quest for information. In a highly organized community, such as the police department, it may mean the police chief or the director of community relations. Often it's not quite that simple. I once set out to interview several elderly Indians on a reservation for an article on Indian legends. To obtain their cooperation I approached one of them, considered a leader of the others, through an intermediary, his daughter-in-law, whom I knew personally. He was skeptical. Negotiations were delicate. I wrote letters and the daughter-in-law made frequent phone calls urging his cooperation. Finally the old man relented and agreed to see me. He never showed up. Three subsequent appointments were made and broken by him. Finally on the fifth try we did meet and the conversation proceeded amicably. I did not broach the topic of legends until late in the discussion. When I did, he protested that he didn't know any myths. "Well, who does?" I asked. He listed several names, and I said I'd love to talk with them. "Okay," he said suddenly. "We'll go tonight." And we did. When one woman protested that she couldn't tell a legend in English, the old man even arranged to supply a translator. My patience paid off. I could never have accomplished any of this without the man's help.

Objectivity

Most communities (that is, groups of people, not merely municipalities) are divided into two or more factions: labor-management, young-old, progressive-conservative, and so forth. When dealing with factions, the interviewer must be especially cautious to maintain an attitude of interested professionalism—which means objectivity. A sociologist (Miller, 1952) suggests that "over-rapport" with one faction hampered his study of labor union personnel. He'd been told a lot of confidential things on a "friend-to-friend" basis by one faction. Now he had a serious dilemma. If he continued the friend-to-friend rapport he could not ask potentially embarrassing or antagonistic questions. But if he tried suddenly to be more aloof and objective, he'd breed distrust. You'll find in such circumstances

that it's better to be a "friendly journalist" than a "journalistic friend"—
you must, in short, maintain a stance of professional objectivity.

Opportunities to Learn

The first of your project interviews will be learning experiences. I once
interviewed a group of police detectives about their techniques of interrogation. The first refused to divulge any techniques on the ground that
the published answers would enable suspects to resist the ploys of the
investigator. I felt this was silly, since the article was intended for an
academic journal. I came better prepared with the second detective. I
read books on interrogation beforehand, and I cited *already published*
techniques as pump primers. This point may argue against starting your
first interview at the top with the most important person. You can compromise by starting at the top with a brief explanatory conversation that
will gain approval for the other interviews you plan to conduct. Then you
can go back later for a longer talk.

Collecting Bits and Pieces

What one respondent doesn't tell you another will. What often evolves
from multiple interviews is a kind of mosaic of information. You look for
colorful patterns built of bits and pieces from each interview. Therefore,
taking copious notes is less important than keeping alert for one or two
colorful fragments. An hour-long interview may yield one anecdote or one
fact you didn't already know. That's all you should expect. This should
enable you to relax and enjoy the conversation; this attitude, in turn,
will bring more informality and candor.

Voluntary Informants and Manipulators

As is true with news beat coverage (next chapter), volunteers often come
forth with information and ideas once word gets around that you're on
the job. They may have ulterior motives, of course, and their information
should be judged in that light. James Michener, researching the 1970
Kent State University shooting incident, reports that he often received
late-night phone calls by persons wanting a secret rendezvous to convey
information.

Trading Information

A conscientious interviewer frequently reaches the point where he knows
more about a topic than any single informant. You find people granting

you interviews largely to learn what you've found out. Your candor encourages their candor. Short of violating confidences, this appears to be an equitable tradeoff. An anthropologist, Clyde Kluckholn, once suggested, "Many human beings consciously or unconsciously resent being 'pumped dry.' If the anthropologist will tell enough stories about his own personal life to at least give the illusion that a swapping of information is going on, the subject will frequently be freer and less guarded." Eventually you find yourself giving a lot more than you get. Perhaps that would be the time to consider sitting down at the typewriter to begin your article. Former *Redbook* editor André Fontaine suggests that the magazine writer is through researching when his sources begin to repeat each other. But he warns that beginning writers are inclined to do too little research, not too much. "So the final rule is, interview, interview, interview" (from *The Art of Writing Nonfiction*).

Systematic Observation

The journalist is a trained observer. He routinely notes down such items as what a person is wearing, the details of a room that might figure in the story (such as the police squad room), and perhaps even snippets of conversation overheard or activities observed as people get together informally. A valuable book that will stimulate both your imagination and your skills in systematic observation (Webb et al., *Unobtrusive Measures*) describes many interesting projects. In one a man walked each night 22 blocks up Broadway in New York, noting the nature of conversations he could overhear. Among his findings from 174 conversations was that "talk of persons of the opposite sex" was heard in 8 percent of the man-to-man conversations and 44 percent of the woman-to-woman conversations. Another project found that one group of typists made a lot more errors copying highly erotic material than another group copying a text on mineralogy.

Informal Observation and Interviewing

The author of a *Reader's Digest* article on intuition spent much research time simply bringing up the topic whenever he met people socially. Almost everyone had had some experience with it and related interesting anecdotes. They didn't even know they were being "interviewed." Magazine writers find this grassroots kind of research valuable because the magazines for which they write are often oriented to reader service rather than public affairs. They try to help readers with everyday problems, such as planning meals, buying a new house, or raising children. I spent eight years, for example, "researching" an article on child care, simply by observing my own children. Through this observation I felt I had gained a worthwhile insight: kids are physically and psychologically tougher than most parents think. So I wrote an article (*Parents'*, April 1973) suggesting that parents shouldn't protect their children from the kind of physical hardships that will offer them a chance to mature. My eight years of "interviews" were nothing more than everyday parent-child conversations.

This kind of interviewing and observation does have one major pitfall. I once suggested to a bachelor friend that he undertake to write an article about "The Southern Woman" since he appeared to have more than academic interest in them. Ten years have elapsed and my still-unattached friend has not produced a single word of copy on the topic.

"Still doing research," he explained cheerfully the last time I inquired.

SEVEN

Getting Established On a News Beat

Q. Hi, sergeant, what's new?
A. Nothing. Same old routine.

Nothing is so intimidating to the young reporter as facing for the first time a bureaucratic iceberg such as city hall or the county courthouse. He finds it populated with strange people who speak an exotic jargon. Garbage dumps are called sanitary landfills. Filling one is known as solid waste disposal. Meetings and hearings and arraignments are laden with opaque phrases such as *first and second readings . . . declaring an emergency . . . defendant then and there being did then and there unlawfully . . . against the statutes made and provided . . . against the peace and dignity of the State . . .*

How is he ever to understand it, let alone write about it? Some critics suggest that a lot of reporters don't even try—that they are so out of touch with the bureaucrats who handle the public's business and spend its money that reporters literally don't know what's new. The sharp indictment of the performance of American news media is not new. A. J. Liebling wrote in the *New Yorker* in 1948 that the American press reminded him of a "gigantic, super-modern fish cannery, a hundred floors high, capitalized at eleven billion dollars, and with tens of thousands of workers standing ready at the canning machine, but relying for its raw material on an inadequate number of handline fishermen in leaky rowboats" ("Goodbye, M.B.I.," *New Yorker,* 7 February, 1948).

Some evidence suggests that the disparity is even greater today. The fish cannery has become even more gleaming and gigantic with a dazzling array of computerized electronics that whisks words into print at awesome speed. The work of the handline fishermen, meanwhile, is as sporadic and capricious as ever. You may find hundreds of them, their leaky rowboats jammed together, frenetically competing for a single fish such as coverage of the Patricia Hearst case. Meanwhile broad expanses of potentially productive fishing grounds remain uncovered. Some newer trends—investigative reporting, depth reporting, team reporting—have tended to direct the reporter's work into special projects and away from the routine, day-to-day contact with news sources. To jargon, news bureaucracy, and sporadic coverage you can add the problem of young reporters who don't have the foggiest notion of where to look for news and how to harvest it. At this point you may wonder if the news media have any contact with reality at all.

The city editor of a fifty thousand-circulation West Coast daily complains about his young reporters: "I can't get them out of the office. They don't know how to fish for news or get people to call them with tips and ideas. I'm constantly nagging them—'if you've got a spare hour go over and talk with the city manager. Talk about the weather, the city, its problems, the manager's dreams for a better community.' The reporters don't like to do that. They think they have to have a specific question to ask or else they're wasting time."

The city manager in that same community says, "The reporters used to come in all the time and we'd just sit and shoot the breeze over coffee. They've stopped doing that, and I don't know why. I guess they think I'm too busy. Well, I *am* busy but not too busy to see reporters. I learn something from the contact, too, and that makes it worthwhile."

These comments add up to a basic principle of beat coverage. Writing the news requires keeping in touch with reality. And that means ferreting out information by keeping in regular contact with persons who are in a position to participate in or at least monitor daily events of public importance or interest. Such people are usually known as news sources, and they can be desk sergeants at police headquarters or presidents, kings, and commissars.

"The most profitable relationship between reporter and news sources," said John M. Hightower of the Associated Press, "is that which produces recurrent interviews. To be thus continuous and productive, the relationship must be based on respect and fair-dealing on both sides." Another Washington journalist, Jim G. Lucas of Scripps-Howard, said he was told upon arriving in the capital that "there are two ways of getting news in this town. You kick it out of them. Or you charm it out of them. . . . Take your time. Decide. Are you a kicker or a charmer?" (Both quoted in Harrall's *Keys to Successful Interviewing*.)

Lucas concluded that he was neither. His techniques were more basic: honesty and fairness. In short, integrity. One further quality for the beat reporter needs to be cited, something Joseph and Stewart Alsop called "decent self-respect" (*The Reporter's Trade*). It means that you're honest, fair, open-minded, and tolerant—but you're nobody's patsy. That's an important quality because the beat reporter invariably encounters a few less honest, less tolerant persons, often in positions of high power and prestige, who will try to manipulate what the reporter writes. Some try by oozing charm, others by coercion, still others by deceit.

Beat reporting is by no means limited to newspapers or broadcast stations. A "shelter" magazine, such as *Better Homes* or *Sunset,* regularly covers such sources as architects, home economists, horticulturalists, research agencies, and others who deal in the home-food-gardening specialties of the magazine. Still another "beat" is the long series of interviews done by writers of articles and nonfiction books. Truman Capote "covered" Holcomb, Kansas, and the careers of two killers for six years in preparing his nonfiction work, *In Cold Blood.* Even a novelist's work might occasionally be defined as beat coverage, as for example, Arthur Hailey's interviews with banking and lending agency personnel for his novel, *The Moneychangers.*

THE NEWS REPORTER'S WORK DEFINED

Of all these areas of reporting, however, the work of the news reporter remains the least understood. This may be because the definition of news is the most ambiguous. The beat reporter must be especially sensitive to this definition, however, because his success depends on his ability to distinguish news from the din of meaningless public activity, just as a prospector must separate gold from raw ore. What, then, is news?

Wise journalists duck that question, suggests a *Washington Post* writer, Charles B. Seib. "Those less wise offer definitions ranging from the inane —'news is what happens'—to the arrogant—'news is what we say it is.' " Perhaps the trouble is that definitions tend to get lost in the complexity of modern society. For an adequate explanation within the context of beat coverage, one must return to an earlier, simpler time. In 1907 John L. Given suggested in his book, *Making a Newspaper,* that newspapers do not keep a watch on all mankind. They station watchers at "a comparatively small number of places where it is made known when the life of anyone in the city departs from ordinary paths or when events worth talking about occur." These watch points include police headquarters, the county clerk's office, the fire department, the courts, city hall, the legislature, Congress, the White House.

The dual concept—departing from ordinary paths, and events worth talking about—belongs in the definition of news. A Honolulu newspaperman and author, Bob Krauss, suggests this example: You pass ten houses on your way to work, and everything is routine at nine of them. The tenth is on fire, and there's a fist fight on the front lawn. Which would *you* talk about when you got to the office?

People also tend to talk about people, especially when their activities depart from routine. The more prominent the person, the more talk about him. For years John Smith, the community's leading banker, has lived a routinely exemplary life. Then one day he beats up his wife, sets his house afire, steals a hundred thousand dollars from the bank, and skips town. The newspaper learns of these extraordinary departures through its watchers at police headquarters and the fire department. Smith probably will be seen again in other news channels: in the courts as he's indicted for robbery or sued for divorce, at police headquarters when he is arrested, at bankruptcy court as his bank goes out of business. All of these are news channels where the lives of people touch base with authority.

One definition, then, suggests that news depicts something definite occurring in unmistakable form: a fire, an arrest, a death, a riot, a bill in Congress, a vote, a speech, the remarks of a famous person. In his classic *Public Opinion* Walter Lippmann said in 1922,

> News is not a mirror of social conditions but the report of an aspect that has obtruded itself. The news does not tell you how the seed is germinating in the ground, but it may tell you when the first sprout breaks the ground. It may even tell you what somebody says is happening to the seed under ground. It may tell you that the sprout did not come up at the time it was expected. The more points, then, at which any happening can be fixed, objectified, measured, named, the more points there are at which news can occur.

It is necessary, then, for the reporter to identify those points in his news beat watching. Some reporters are better at this than others. "If a journalist sees a building with a dangerous list," explains Lippmann, "he does not have to wait until it falls into the street in order to recognize news."

Less perceptive reporters may have to wait for the crash. Some are unable to see it even then. A legendary story tells of a cub reporter sent to cover the launching of a ship. He returned empty-handed. The story didn't pan out, he told his editor. "Something went wrong and the ship stuck on the ways. They hope to get her into the water tomorrow." The reporter had failed to perceive it as an ironic departure from ordinary paths.

Many basic concepts remain the same as in the time of Given and the young Lippmann, though today writers see some ordinary paths as having a firm place in the definition of news. This is certainly true of those ordinary pathways that touch the lives of people. That inflation steadily eats away at earning power may be routine, yet it remains a matter of public interest and importance. So do unemployment, pollution, energy, and violent crime. So does the routine work of the mayor, the city council, the legislature, the Congress. Though the work may be routine, it affects people's taxes, living conditions, and their relationships with those elected to run the government.

Therefore a further definition of news should include the identification of "milestones" along the road to social, economic, and political progress. Government agencies, after all, did not spring from nowhere. They were formed to cope with societal problems, usually very specific ones: crime, contagious disease, unemployment, education of the young, injustices, and many others. The public has an interest—indeed, a profound right—in knowing whether the goals are being met.

The beat reporter, then, works to define some objective point at which it becomes appropriate to report the progress. Would it be an annual report? A speech by an official? The firing of an administrator? The announcement of a new budget or an increase in taxes? Any of these can be the point that defines the trend. It is not always necessary to report progress. Let's say a new crime fighting unit of elite officers has been established in your city. It sends officers to areas of high crime rates in burglary, violence, and armed robbery. The police reporter makes periodic checks. How effective is this unit? Is the burglary rate dropping? How many arrests have been made? It would be difficult to imagine *not* finding a news story in the work of such a unit. Suppose you ask the officer in charge, "What's happening with the special unit?" He replies, "Nothing." If he really means it, you have a story: No progress is being made despite the efforts of an elite and expensive corps of officers. That's a newsworthy twist of irony, to say the least.

A List of News Beats

Just where are these watch stations, the news beats where reporters keep an eye on the news channels? A typical newspaper serving a middle-sized U.S. city might split them up like this:

Emergency services Police and fire departments, hospitals, medical examiner, ambulance services, jails, Coast Guard

Courts State, federal, and local courts; also appellate courts, juvenile, probate, and bankruptcy courts

City services City hall, city council, municipal agencies such as civil service, street engineering, waste disposal, planning and zoning, and others

County Tax collection, board of commissioners, welfare, health and sanitation, elections, environmental control, housing. State courts are often housed in the county building

State Governor and legislature if the city is also a state capital; otherwise branches of state agencies such as highways, public welfare, corrections, motor vehicle licensing, veterans agencies, and many others.

Federal Post office, immigration service, internal revenue, agricultural agencies, law enforcement and regulatory agencies, military bases

Business Chamber of commerce, business and professional organizations, major local industries (oil in Texas, lumbering in Oregon, sugar in Hawaii), public utilities, media and ad agencies, financial institutions

Sports Professional and interscholastic athletics, outdoor activities, participation sports (golf, tennis, swimming, hiking, mountain climbing, sailing)

Politics Political organizations, individual political leaders, office holders

Education School boards, student activities, colleges, superintendent's office

Social welfare Altruistic organizations, youth agencies, social betterment groups, minority rights groups, United Fund

Agriculture Farm agencies, granges, and other agricultural organizations

Transportation Airports, railroads, waterfront, highways, convention centers, tourist agencies, hotels, airlines

Entertainment Movies and theaters, concerts, books, radio and TV, travel, civic events (fairs, parades, rodeos, etc.)

Science and technology Research agencies, college science departments, museums, archival agencies, medical societies, inventors' groups

Team Reporting

Variations exist from community to community, of course. A recent trend is "team reporting" in which groups of reporters work to cover a broadly defined area such as "Monetary Activities," which include business, finance, labor, transportation, and related activities. This allows deployment of investigators to wherever the need is greatest. It permits several reporters to work on a single story of special importance. But it also tends to diminish the opportunity for one reporter to establish close and effective rapport with his news sources.

The team approach reflects a gradual trend toward "depth reporting" based on more thorough and comprehensive investigations. The problems that concern people do not always fit the artificial categories represented by beats. A reporter, unless he observes broadly and reads widely, may perceive reality in an extremely narrow sense.

Take the demonstrations on college campuses across the country a few years ago, for example. Did that story "belong" to the education reporter? Or the police reporter when cops were called on campus? The political reporter because of political repercussions? Social welfare because minority rights were often at issue? The answer is that all of these areas were involved, and more. Society has grown far too complex to separate reporters into watertight compartments.

Nonetheless, the beat system persists in one form or another, as well it should. *Somebody* has to be out scouting the halls of government and finance and social concern to find out what's going on and how your and my money is being spent.

GETTING STARTED ON A BEAT

Let's assume that you have been placed on the county courthouse beat: county government and the state trial courts. How do you begin? If you're lucky, an experienced reporter will take you around, show you where public documents such as court complaints and petitions are filed, and introduce you to important bureaucrats. But many reporters have had to learn a beat on their own, simply by diving in.

The water is seldom as icy as you think.

The work of the reporter is not confined to those abominable sidewalk interviews you so often see on network TV, nor does the reporter have to resort to clever subterfuges of *Front Page* genre. Plenty of sympathetic and helpful people will come forward to help the reporter, once his motives are understood to be honorable. Their motives are not always so noble. Elected officials are mindful of reelection and the need to keep their names before the public. Other persons may seek revenge against their enemies by offering tips about situations wherein public disclosure may discredit those enemies.

Others—most, in fact—are guided by higher principles. Public agencies often rely on the media for routine announcements, such as a public hearing for the routing of a new highway or for an ordinance to ban public nudity. Agency heads also realize that reports of their activities bring public cooperation and support, as for example a health department's campaign to prevent spread of infectious hepatitis. All agencies are mindful of budget allocations and the role public interest can play in getting an adequate share of the tax dollar. And that ever-present Sword of Damocles, the budget election, forces even the grumpiest of bureaucrats to smile upon reporters occasionally.

A few enlightened agencies—especially those that have employed community relations officers—have concluded that it's unrealistic to assume that all the news about their activities should be favorable. Their reasons may be a little different from yours. They've learned, often the hard way, that it's folly to have their departments portrayed favorably all year long only to face angry voters at a budget election with a request for more tax dollars to "take care of all our problems." *What problems?* All year the media had been reporting that the department was doing an excellent job. Why this sudden eleventh-hour crisis?

The fledgling beat reporter, therefore, may be surprised how warmly he's welcomed. He is sought out as often as he seeks out. He is constantly "tested" with all manner of ideas for publicity. He's bombarded with press releases, tips, suggestions. Pseudo events—ceremonies, press conferences, demonstrations, inspection tours—are staged for his benefit (and for the publicity). Eventually he learns that noisy drum beating by one official may be calculated to distract him from noticing problems in some dark corner. He'll learn to recognize drum beaters, manipulators, and "journalistic street walkers."

The latter are often seen around legislative halls. As one reporter explains it, the "street walker" is a politician who has a bit of information he thinks reporters will want. But he's reluctant to go directly to them: that would be too pushy. So he patrols the legislative hallways provocatively during times when he knows news-hungry reporters are about. Here's a typical conversation:

> Q. Hi, Senator, how're things?
> A. Well, I'm pretty tired. . . .
> Q. Oh, really?
> A. Yeah, I've been up all night working.
> Q. What on?
> A. I've been busy with this important report . . . just finished it . . . it's really gonna blow the lid off—
> Q. (Animated) Oh, yeah? Tell me about it. . . .

Above all the new reporter learns that most news from a beat comes from routine sources requiring little special initiative on his part. Committee meetings, hearings, and caucuses go on day and night, and most are open to reporters. The amount of paper—documents, orders, annual reports, positions papers, public statements, committee reports, minutes—is astounding. The danger is not that the new reporter will return to his office empty-handed and defeated. It is that amid the blizzard of paper he will unwittingly ignore equally deserving but hard-to-get stories from less aggressive agencies. The reporter should resist the temptation to jump for what glitters and should strive to establish a careful system of coverage that insures that no potential sources of information are overlooked.

Often missing from beat coverage amid today's concern for depth reporting is the systematic, periodic, and long-standing contact between the reporter and his sources. The sources include more than agency heads. They include second-echelon personnel. They even include secretaries and janitors, the former because they usually know what's going on and the latter because they empty the wastebaskets and know where the mistakes lie hidden.

Three Sources of News

In the final analysis, then, systematic beat coverage is a three-legged stool. First is news from routine press releases, press conferences, meetings, documents—in short, *source-initiated* material. Second is *reporter-initiated* news: interviews, pursuit of tips and leads and hunches, follow-ups on ongoing projects. The third—and the one too often overlooked—is the news that comes from the *interaction of a reporter and his news source.* This third leg produces a kind of intelligence that neither party could produce alone. Mostly it happens informally. Some reporters call it "coffee cup reporting."

Explains one news source, a state legislator: "We meet over coffee or in the hallways or during breaks in meetings. The reporters just come around and ask what's the scoop on this bill or that issue. I think this is good because reporters can ferret out stories that would not always be appropriate for press releases because they might hurt somebody's feelings. This way the public gets a more candid and realistic story." The legislator wouldn't volunteer certain kinds of touchy information. The reporter doesn't know about it. But informal coffee cup contact allows it to emerge naturally. The reporter simply gets his source in a talking mood, directs the conversation into productive channels, and then listens for the news stories almost sure to emerge in the conversation.

The informal give-and-take is by no means limited to personal contact. Once the first few cups of coffee are consumed and the reporter-source relationship is well established, the phone can be used. Here is one reporter's account (he wrote it down at the end of the conversation) of an actual "fishing expedition" conversation with a woman in charge of community relations at the county courthouse.

Q. What's new?

A. What's new? Well, same old routine.

Q. Ha! That's what they all say. You've heard this story about the reporter who calls up the courthouse and asks what's going on? . . . Well, the county judge answers and says, "There's nothing going on," and quickly hangs up. For once he was right.

Seems the courthouse was on fire and everybody had evacuated the building. So they were all standing around outside doing nothing.

A. Right, right. I get the picture. Hey, I smell smoke!

Q. *What?*

A. No, I'm kidding. You reporters are so *jumpy!* . . . Well, if you want to know what's *not* happening, there's no commissioner's meeting next week.

Q. How come?

A. They're all going to a conference out of town.

Q. Are you going too? Are you going to give a speech?

A. Didn't anybody teach you not to ask two questions at once? Yes. No. I'm going but I'm not speaking. I'm going to attend a session about how to bridge the credibility gap.

Q. No need. We all know you're an honest woman.

A. Except I lie to my husband and my kids and my friends—

Q. But only because you have so many state secrets, stuff that would really blow the lid off if people knew—

A. Well, no, I don't really.

Q. So, anyhow, who *is* going to give a speech? Anybody? Or is that two questions?

A. Three. One of the fellows in the Solid Waste Department—he's talking on "Solid Waste and Energy Production." That means burning garbage for electrical energy in case you didn't know—

Q. I know. Is he for it or against it?

A. For it, I hope.

Q. Well, that's worth a story. I'll call him and find out what he intends to say. So who else is going with you on this boondoggle —er, trip?

A. (Gives details. Conversation turns to another county department, the Juvenile Office.)

Q. I've just about given up on that department. I used to work years ago in another county and got lots of stories from juvenile. Here, nothing.

A. They're very protective here.

Q. Like a mother hen. Someday they'll find they'd like more public support—

A. Say, that reminds me, speaking of the courthourse burning—

Q. Oh, no—

A. Seems that the juvenile department *is* interested in the public— so they've started some kind of educational programs with juvenile officers going out and talking to parents' groups about juvenile problems—what youth is all about today, what to look for in the way of problems, drugs, alcohol. Maybe there's a story there.

Q. Right. Could be. I'll check into it.

This brief but typical fishing expedition netted three stories, one representing some new thoughts on ways to handle disposal of garbage, another on a campaign to enlighten the public about juvenile problems, and a third on cancellation of the commissioners' meeting because of the trip.

The GOSS formula, cited in Chapter 4, also works in these fishing expeditions. By asking about goals and obstacles and solutions, you stand an excellent chance of hitting upon specific problems an agency is attempting to solve. You can play hunches, too. Since fall is a time for contagious diseases, the reporter covering the county health department knows to ask about the possibility of another influenza epidemic. In the conversation similar newsworthy problems may emerge, such as epidemics in venereal disease or infectious hepatitis.

If your initial stories on the beat are accurate and honest, word of your reputation soon gets around. If a crisis comes up—a big public controversy in which officials become tense and anxious—your contacts at the courthouse will help you get the story. After all, they *know* you, and they trust you. It's the other reporters they distrust, the ones who come around only when a crisis is at hand. The officials usually don't tell *them* any more than they just have to.

A reporter's reputation for manipulation and deceit gets around, too. One police reporter persisted in surreptitiously reading unauthorized file material. Recalls a police official: "One day we put a lot of junk in that file, including a fictitious murder. He picked it up and got all excited. We let it go just as far as the news desk, and then we called the editor and told him it was all a hoax. We also told the editor why we'd done it. We didn't have any more trouble."

Universal Questions

Most reporters have devised a set of "sure-fire" questions to use when interviewing an agency head without prior briefing. Here are some samples:

    What kinds of problems cause you greatest concern right now?

    What projects are you working on?

    When members of the public talk with you, what kinds of concern are on their minds? How do you respond?

    What kinds of stories could the paper run to help you meet your goals?

    Are you planning any trips, conferences, speeches, or meetings within the next six weeks? What?

What is your department doing to accommodate to new trends if any? What are these trends?

Do you have a vision for what this department might be doing five or ten years from now?

If you had more money, what new projects would you start?

Do you ever ask yourself, what *should* the department be doing? If so, what?

If, as you suggest, nothing noteworthy is going on, could taxpayers save money by eliminating your department? (Guaranteed to wake up sleepy respondents!)

These are questions to be asked when you are in the dark, but asking uninformed questions is generally ineffectual. Reporters seldom grope in complete darkness. They get suggestions from editors, from colleagues, from reading clips of previous stories done on the agency, from reading about similar work elsewhere. They also read trade publications such as *Law & Order, School Board Journal, American City, Chronicle of Higher Education.* Just skimming through a new book on a subject can inspire stimulating questions. A book tells you that police departments across the country are increasing their activities in community relations. What is your local police department doing? If specific projects have been started, you have a story. If not, perhaps you have a different story that answers the question, "Why not?"

SOME BASIC STEPS ON A NEW BEAT

You've been assigned to a new beat—so now what do you do? I put that question to about a dozen experienced newspaper reporters who'd been rotated onto news beats. Here, in composite form, is what they said.

They often took several days off just to get acquainted. They sometimes wrote letters in advance to agency heads: "I'm new on the beat and I'd like to chat informally with you to make sure the reading public gets the best possible coverage of your activities. . . ."

They read library clips about each agency on the beat.

They visited with public relations officers of various agencies to discuss ideas.

They asked for background information about agencies: annual reports, progress reports, memoranda, scrapbooks. They asked sources to identify books and magazines that might be helpful.

They often made on-site inspections of projects and facilities. One woman spent a day in the state penitentiary. Reporters took helicopter rides over highway and harbor construction projects.

They began keeping calendars or "future books," systematically recording all forthcoming events: speeches, meetings, expected dates of announcements for opening or completing projects. Often they asked a source if he'd "help me with my calendar" by referring to his own calendar for important events in the future. That alone brought ideas for stories. Even tentative dates go into the calendar: "We hope to have this new juvenile shelter home started sometime next December," says an executive. The reporter notes it down.

They placed themselves on every conceivable mailing list for newsletters, brochures, catalogues, press releases, reports, announcements.

They began monitoring bulletin boards.

They asked for suggestions and criticisms of past performance. "What do *you* think would make a good story? . . . What kinds of things have we been missing in the past?"

They began to attend public meetings, often as much for tips and ideas as for coverage of the meeting itself. They found it an excellent way to meet important people.

They asked sources to let them know when something interesting happens: "Call me anytime." They left a printed card with their name and phone number. They tried to define "news," and they gave specific ideas of stories they'd like to know about: announcements, new appointments, visiting dignitaries, problems, trends, issues, projects started or completed, or "anything a little out of the ordinary."

They sought to defuse any hostilities left over from another reporter's work or the paper's editorial policy.

They asked for names of others who would make good news contacts.

Eventually—surprisingly soon, most said—they were sought out by persons volunteering to be informal sources or "inside tipsters." They are people who, for reasons ranging from interest in honest government to in-house political revenge, offer tips about problems or delicate situations you'd never learn from agency heads.

They learned where bureaucrats congregate informally: the office cafeteria for coffee, a local restaurant, a cocktail bar, and they gradually eased their way into the circle. They did the same at coffee hours for secretaries and clerks.

They kept an open mind, especially when dealing with people they don't normally associate with. A self-defined "square" says she had no trouble getting information from radical students during a campus crisis: "I just tried to be fair and not misquote them, and that seemed to be all they asked." Another middle-aged woman visited a series of hippie communes with great trepidation at first. But she found warm acceptance. "They told me that no reporters had ever tried to talk with them before," she reported. "I think they considered me a groovy old chick."

They sought opportunities to chat informally with anybody and everybody, including underlings. They drank a lot of coffee.

And what if, in spite of your best efforts, a source remains uncoopera-
tive? One observer, Leon V. Sigal, suggests in his study, *Reporters and
Officials,* that much "bargaining" goes on between journalists and their
sources. Experienced reporters confirm this. Write a favorable story about
a bureaucrat and you stand a better chance of getting tips, leaks, and
exclusive interviews in return. However, any experienced official knows
that refusal to cooperate can result in greater risk of having unfavorable
stories written about him as the reporter seeks alternate sources of
information. A balance of power exists, and it is not always delicate. A
county judge once threatened an editor, "You publish that story and you'll
never get another word of news out of this office." The editor countered,
"You pull a news blackout on us, and you'll have the damnedest public
fight of your life." The judge backed down.

Although occasions will arise when a reporter must use leverage to
secure public information from public officials, he'll find it wise to do so
in moderation and only when all else fails. The news reporter who deals
honestly and openly with his sources seldom has to resort to such devices.
He'll find alternate sources of information, often from individuals within
the recalcitrant bureaucrat's own department. These people tend to be
as impatient with him as the reporter is. Conversely, the "power of the
press," used ruthlessly, can breed fear and contempt among sources far in
excess of whatever short-run gains it may accomplish. If you are going
to err in front of thousands of readers, you'd be wise to err on the side of
truth, fairness, and honesty.

INTERVIEWING BY PHONE

Once he has become acquainted with the people on the beat, the reporter
turns more and more to the telephone, particularly for routine news. Most
public officials do not mind; they're used to conducting business by phone.
For them it's quicker, more efficient, more impersonal (no need for the
social amenities of a face-to-face contact). For the reporter the phone
offers tremendous advantages: no need for time-consuming crosstown trips,
no need to get dressed up (a relief for the person who prefers to work in
casual clothes). Use of a shoulder clip for the phone frees both your hands
for notetaking, and you can take notes faster on a typewriter or video
display terminal. You can keep your notes, clippings, articles, and other
reference materials at your fingertips, conveniently spread out on your
desk. Best of all, you can touch base with several different sources in the
time it would take for just one face-to-face interview.

Reporters for national magazines and newspapers have developed long distance phone interviewing to a fine art. The telephone has a high priority in the minds of many busy executives. They will interrupt almost anything to answer the phone, particularly if the call is long distance. A reporter for a Washington-based trade paper, the *Chronicle of Higher Education,* finds it effective to announce over the phone, "This is Jack Magarrell, *calling from Washington, D.C. . . .*" It gets him quickly through secretaries and into key executive offices.

Indispensable as it may be for routine news gathering, the telephone is considered by many to be ineffective for feature or personality interviews. This idea deserves a closer look, however. The telephone is surprisingly effective for interviews dealing with intimate detail. In some circumstances, people feel less threatened talking into an impersonal instrument precisely because it helps *not* to see a human reaction. A sensitive person discussing a traumatic experience might easily be unnerved by so subtle a reaction as an averted glance. The very weakness of the telephone, its impersonality, can be a strength.

Support for this view comes from a bizarre source. In Honolulu a man telephoned dozens of women, identifying himself as a doctor engaged in research on sex patterns. He asked for and often received intimate details of their sexual experiences. Only in retrospect did some women become suspicious enough to call the medical association, where they learned that the man was a fraud. The women were charmed, they explained, by his warm telephone personality; they characterized him as a "skilled interviewer."

Whether your use of the telephone is for feature or routine news, local or distant, these simple courtesies will help ease the way to effective interviewing.

1. Speak clearly and distinctly. And calmly. Try to put a brisk but amiable and friendly quality into your voice, which is the only means you have to establish rapport.

2. Identify yourself and your purpose quickly and succinctly.

3. Unless the call is to be brief, indicate the possible duration of the interview ("perhaps fifteen minutes") because you don't know what you're interrupting. Suggest that you will gladly call back later at a more appropriate time. You may not suggest that, of course, if you have had difficulty getting through or if you suspect the respondent will be reluctant to talk.

4. You may certainly make icebreaker remarks and personal asides if they are brief. Such remarks usually come after the purpose of the call has been made clear.

5. Don't allow long unexplained silences on the phone. Notetaking is one reason for interviewer silence: explain that you'll need "just a mo-

ment to note down what you're saying." If you take notes on a noisy typewriter, you may want to warn the respondent (particularly an inexperienced one) about the clacking noise in the background.

6. Since the respondent can't see you, you must provide verbal cues of response: "uh-huh" or "okay" or a grunt that suggests you haven't fallen asleep.

7. When interviewing on a sensitive topic, you may need to provide credentials and references, naming mutual acquaintances, if possible, who will vouch for the authenticity of your purpose. Sometimes just arranging for such an interview calls for the help of an intermediary.

WHEN YOU'RE UNPREPARED

Whether on a beat or (more likely) on general assignment, persons who report for newspapers or broadcast stations will conduct interviews for which they have had little or no time to prepare. Some journalists love the challenge of it—"It's like playing twenty questions," explains one. "You might as well confess your unpreparedness," suggests another. "Don't make a big thing of it—just say, I'm sorry, I haven't had time to read your book."

If you are truly unprepared, the solution to your problem is simpler than you might suspect. You do what any good quarterback would do in a tight situation, fourth down deep in his own territory. You punt. That is, you encourage the other person to carry the conversational ball. You play a quiet defensive game, using the time the respondent is talking to (1) plan strategy for the interview and (2) pick up cues for follow-up questions. To do this, you say something—anything—calculated to get the other person talking. It doesn't have to be brilliant: "What brings you to River City, Senator?" or "Did you have a good trip?" or "I see by the papers they're fighting in Congress again over the budget." You are simply seeking a common denominator to get the conversation started.

Once he starts to talk, you encourage him to continue. You stay alert to anything said that may offer clues to further questions or comments. You employ what ultimately is the best preparation of all—a lively curiosity, an interest in all kinds of people, and a general knowledge gained through extensive reading.

Of course, you are seldom totally without advance clues. A typical newsroom crisis runs like this. The city editor hangs up the phone and calls you over (or comes to your desk). "My gosh," he says, "they're having a conference at the Public Utility office about solar energy, and they've got this expert up from California, fellow by the name of Jones. He's got a spare thirty minutes right now, so let's get an interview. Ah, sorry to spring this on you suddenly, but . . . ."

No use protesting why this wasn't thought of a week or even two hours ago. You have sufficient background if you've taken the trouble to keep up with the news. You've read frequent reports about the energy crisis, so you wonder whether solar energy can play a significant role in easing that crisis. Obvious questions suggest themselves. Can solar energy be used to heat homes? Can or will it be used in the form of power-producing plants to provide energy for whole communities? What will it cost? What about areas where the sun doesn't shine? Is research being conducted on the subject? Where? With what conclusions? What problems hinder the use of solar energy? What are some solutions?

(It took me a minute and thirty seconds to think up the above questions and write them down. Better ones occur to me now, later, but I'll let the originals stand as a kind of monument to what an ordinary guy can accomplish with ninety seconds of preparation.)

All experienced journalists have stock questions to use in such emergencies. Here are some of the common ones:

How do you feel about _____? (Fill in winning an award, losing your husband in the mine disaster, being released from prison, winning the election, etc. Frankly I hate the question, particularly on TV, and sincerely hope you never have to use it.)

How did you get started (or first become interested) in _____? (The chronological approach often elicits lengthy response, thus giving you a chance to get your bearings.)

What are some of the major problems (trends, changes) in _____? (The blank should be filled with a subject about which the respondent is an expert: world affairs for a statesman, Washington politics for a Congressman, schools for an educator.)

What do you see as the future of _____? What would you like to tell the public about _____? What issues in _____ do you expect to see emerging in the months ahead? What are people talking about in _____ (respondent's place of residence or field of expertise)?

The list could go on, but perhaps you get the idea. All these questions are punting maneuvers designed to let the respondent carry the ball. It's a lousy—not to mention lazy—way of interviewing. In the crush of daily news reporting, however, sometimes it's the only way.

But if you have ten minutes to prepare, how about reading clips from the library? Or call an expert at a nearby university for advice on what to ask. Call the reference room of the community library (or pay a small toll charge to call a larger library). Call an appropriate agency (for example, for your interview with the secretary of agriculture, coming up in five minutes, call the county agricultural agent for advice and suggestions).

Ideally, a well-organized beat system will solve many such problems. The agriculture secretary would be interviewed by the agriculture beat reporter and the solar energy expert by the science reporter. Today's society is too complex to leave the reporting of it to amateurs.

EIGHT

Interviewing for Broadcast

Q. Mr. Mayor, will you be having any statement today on the mass resignation of
three hundred police officers, or the labor
strike in the Sanitation Department, or
the grand jury indictments of three of
your most trusted assistants for embezzle-
ment, or last night's dynamite explosion
that all but demolished City Hall?

A. Nope.

Q. Thank you, sir. Have a good day.

A good broadcast interview is "like floating a river—you hit exciting rapids
and peaceful deep pools—and you never know for sure what's around
the next bend." This is a conclusion reached by Margaret Laine, a
graduate student at the University of Oregon in 1976, who undertook a
research project on the topic of broadcast interviewing. She interviewed
twenty radio and television journalists throughout Oregon and she read
widely on the subject. She found several important distinctions between
interviewing for print and interviewing for broadcast. She also concluded
that broadcast interviewers often do not pay sufficient attention to those
distinctions. Instead, they tend to conduct print interviews for broadcast.
In short, they do not adapt their interviewing techniques to the unique
qualities of broadcast, particularly television, which provides multidimensional qualities of communication wherein facial expressions and body
language can sometimes say more about a person or situation than all the
words exchanged. Laine explains:

The broadcast interview should not be a print interview with pictures or sound added. Ideally, it should transmit some information, some impression, some *something* that can only be transmitted through the electronic media. It should tap the unique advantages of its medium. Very rarely does this happen.[1]

What too often happens, she explains, is that broadcast interviewers, vaguely aware that the medium is uniquely capable of communicating "feelings," end up merely asking about them: "How do you *feel* about the fire that destroyed your home and sent your baby to the hospital?" Laine continues:

> Larry Wissbeck of KGW–TV, Portland, suggests how an actuality might both catch the "feel" and elicit some new information: "Say the mayor has just announced that from now on all policemen will be authorized to carry shotguns in police cars. There are two things you could get out of an interview with the mayor—auxiliary comments getting to the real 'why' behind the decision, and a feel for the dynamics of the decision—how he feels about it. The expression on his face and the sweat popping on his forehead are information, too. And that's why you interview over the air."
>
> Of course, both potential areas of information could be totally missed if the reporter went barging into the mayor's office, thrust a microphone in his face, and *asked* him how he felt about the decision. The mayor's feelings about the situation are more likely to come out in the process of the reporter's sensitive, probing questions that suggest an understanding of the situation as a whole.

For better or for worse, most of what the public knows about interviewing comes from broadcast: the harsh confrontation tactics of a Mike Wallace, the amiable sensitivity of a Dick Cavett, the aloof hostility of a *Meet the Press* session, the gross tactics of the local newscaster who thrusts a mike beneath the nose of a distraught crime victim: "How does it *feel* to be held hostage for four hours in a bank vault?"

Most of the suggestions in this book can be adapted to broadcast interviewing. Such principles as defining a purpose, conducting background research, opening an interview on an innocuous or ego-supportive note, and establishing conversational rapport are largely the same. Further, many interviews done by radio and TV personnel are routine information gathering, not intended for broadcast. Those do not differ essentially from routine newsgathering interviews for newspapers.

It is on-the-air interviewing—either live or taped for later broadcast—where differences become apparent. One of these differences has been dramatized by I. E. Fang in his book, *Television News*. He characterizes a news conference with print reporters as dull and listless. Then the TV

---

[1] Margaret Laine, "Broadcast Interviewing Handbook," 1976. All the passages quoted from this unpublished paper are reprinted by permission of the author.

reporters show up. The respondent comes quickly to life. He engages in five minutes of fast-paced, scintillating discussion with the TV reporters. Then they depart, and the discussion sinks back to its listless state. The point is confirmed by many print reporters themselves—"The guy just blossoms out in front of a camera," says one—and some have even purchased small tape recorders, hoping to use them to capture some of the élan of the broadcast interview.

The main point of difference, however, is not whether one interviewing method is dull and the other lively. It's simply that broadcast interviewing involves a "performance" characteristic. The interviewer must do more than ask questions. You must establish an atmosphere of spirited rapport that allows the respondent (or "guest") to forget cameras, lights, time cues, and stage fright and deliver his best personality in a lively conversation that will inform, entertain, and communicate a "feel" for the personality.

Broadcast interviews come in two basic types, "extended" and "quickie."

THE EXTENDED BROADCAST INTERVIEW

This interview lasts anywhere from ten to ninety minutes, usually with a celebrity or newsmaker, live or taped. It is essentially a conversational interchange. It is usually done in a broadcast studio, though viewers are often treated to imaginative exceptions: a 747 pilot in his cockpit aloft, a fashion designer behind the scenes of a busy fashion show, a farmer on a hilltop overlooking a panoramic vista of miles and miles of wheat fields. Whatever the site, the interviewer must be skilled in phrasing questions succinctly and sometimes provocatively. As a reporter, you must not only know the topic under discussion but you must know beforehand the nature of the personality you're dealing with. The dominant personality must be aggressively pursued with questions lest the show become a monologue. The submissive personality must be brought out by gentle questions and sensitive listening.

All of this must occur amid the sometimes chaotic confusion of the television studio: the lights, the two or more cameras, the sometimes frantic time cues from a floor director ("hurry it up," "stretch it out," "five minutes to go," "three minutes," "thirty seconds," etc.). Confesses one journalist in describing her first television interview: "I was so worried about time cues and which camera to face that I forgot to listen to the answers to my questions. It's hard to ask follow-up questions when you have no idea what you're following up." So the responsibility and pressure on the broadcast interviewer are enormous. The interviewer must nonetheless remain relaxed and informal, knowing that any show of nervousness is likely to be reflected in the guest's behavior.

While the print interviewer might be expected to interview just about anybody, the broadcast interviewer must be more selective, at least for lengthy live interviews. Some broadcasters have even identified "poor risk" categories—people who don't come across well on the air. A radio network official once cited three of them: scientists, doctors, and educators. Clearly some prescreening is important for all but perfunctory interviews; no television viewer is so sadistic as to enjoy seeing a human being suffer from agonizing stage fright. Some guests have been so nervous that they were literally unable to speak. It is, of course, the responsibility of the interviewer to try to relax those nervous souls who do get on the air.

Intense preparation is the key, along with emphasis on whatever "human" qualities a broadcaster can manage to squeeze out of an essentially artificial situation. These include nonjudgmental listening, an alert body posture, smiles, nods, even "listening" with the eyes. The skilled interviewer also knows (through preparation and preinterview conversation) the kinds of questions likely to stimulate pleasant and spirited answers. He can use those to control the tempo and atmosphere of the conversation. Explains an Oregon broadcaster, Ken Crockett: "Your guest is the police chief. Crime is up by over 50 percent and you want to know why. Instead of immediately putting the man on the defensive by demanding an explanation, you ask him instead about the force's new police cars. He likes to talk about that: he brightens, talks animatedly. Then you hit him with 'just how are your new police cars likely to affect the rising crime rate?' "

Preparation will allow you to put into your questions enough background to educate the audience. Don't ask, "Senator, what do you think of the governor's new education tax proposal?" Both you and your guest know what you're talking about, but the audience probably does not. For its benefit you must rephrase your question, starting with an enlightening statement: "As you know, the governor's new tax proposal places a three percent tax on hotel and motel rooms to raise money for public schools. . . . What is your view of that proposal?"

Similarly, a remark by the guest that is rambling and incoherent requires a summarizing comment by the interviewer: "As I understand it, then, you are saying . . ." Your summary may be wrong, but the guest will hasten to clarify, usually more succinctly.

The broadcast interviewer, in short, must "edit" on the spot on behalf of the unseen audience. The print interviewer can write clarifications into his article. The broadcast interviewer must never allow the conversation to become so esoteric that it excludes the audience. Explains Oregon TV reporter Larry Wissbeck: "If it's missing the audience it's a failure. It's like a highly intellectual debate between William F. Buckley and Henry Kissinger. They are the only ones who have any idea of what they're talking about. That's not journalism."

But the broadcast interviewer must not go too far in the opposite direction, using trite or elementary questions. You waste tremendous air time asking, say, a reformed alcoholic such questions as "When did you start drinking? . . . When did you stop? . . . How much did you drink per week?" Such points can be secured through prebroadcast interviews and incorporated into the introduction of your guest: "John Doe is a reformed alcoholic who stopped drinking ten years ago after consuming the equivalent of fifteen bathtubsful of whiskey, gin, wine, and beer over a period of fifteen years. . . ." Having dispensed with such details, you can proceed right to the heart of the subject.

Going to the heart means you'll get to the "bomb" or potentially sensitive or embarrassing questions more quickly than you would in a print interview. That's because broadcast interviews tend to be short and fragmented with commercial breaks and because both audience and respondent have come to expect the tough controversial questions from broadcast interviews. They become impatient with pussyfooting. Sometimes the respondent becomes tense and nervous.

However, broadcasters usually open their interviews with easy, innocuous, pleasant questions. Ken Crockett explains why. "If I open with a hard question and the man gets off to a bad start—he stumbles around with it, he can't pull his words together, the sweat starts pouring off his forehead—he may never recover, may *never* relax. If, on the other hand, he handles an easy question well, he immediately begins to loosen up. He thinks, 'This isn't so bad—I *can* do it!' "

Should rehearsal precede a broadcast interview? Definitely not, say most broadcasters. Rehearsal leads to stilted conversation. Some preinterview discussion is desirable, however, to establish rapport and size up the guest. Perhaps routine bits of information or clarification can be secured at this time: they will help you to ask better questions on the air. Some general discussion of the areas to be covered might be in order. Of course the guest should be told at the time of initial contact what the interview is to be about. He might want to decline. Or he may wish to consult some documents, talk with colleagues, or think through some answers. It probably helps to let him know the first question, presumably an easy one, so that he can prepare some remarks that will ease him through those first tense seconds on the air. Experienced interviewers advise against telling the guest any of the remaining questions; it destroys spontaneity. If a guest starts to tell you an interesting story prior to the broadcast, stop him. Tell him to save it for the broadcast. If he has told it once, he may think to himself during the broadcast, "He certainly doesn't want to hear *that* story again." If you want *really* spontaneous answers on the air, you'll ask spontaneous questions: those improvised during the interview itself.

That means listening carefully, of course. It also means interrupting. Some respondents tend to ramble; others try to dominate. The interviewer should not hesitate to cut in with a question or comment: "He's got to stop for a breath *sometime,*" suggests a radio journalist. Some broadcasters tell respondents beforehand, "Keep your answers short and rely on me for followup questions—it will produce a more lively conversation and the audience will enjoy it more." Barbara Walters defends her frequent interruptions when she was on the *Today* show:

> If I were doing a written interview I wouldn't interrupt. I could sit back and listen for hours. But on *Today,* interviews run from four to a maximum of twelve minutes. Guests usually don't understand how short that is, so they may start to tell a long story. So I'm acting as an editor. I am getting time cues: I know there is one minute left or 30 seconds and the person has not made his point, so I interrupt to give him an opportunity to say what he has to say. It's not for my benefit. But it would upset me and the guest if he didn't get to make his point. (Shalit in *Ladies' Home Journal,* November 1975.)

Should the broadcast interviewer use notes or write out questions, especially on TV? Frequent shuffling through notes and papers during the interview is annoying to respondent and audience alike because it distracts from the conversation. It even suggests that the interviewer isn't listening. If prepared questions are used they might be written on a single card and left on a stand or table, in view but not handled. The interviewer should pay as much attention as possible to the respondent. He also must avoid the natural tendency to keep saying "uh-huh," "okay," or "hmmm." It annoys viewers. Use eye contact, smiles, and nods of the head.

Successful broadcast interviewers are unique in their styles and thus worthy of comment. Dick Cavett usually starts an interview innocuously, then creeps into sensitive questions so subtly that most guests answer glibly with hardly a second thought. Mike Wallace is brilliant and tough and abrasive—a showman, to say the least. As a result he sometimes brings out interesting qualities in guests that the public hasn't seen before, often tough and defiant qualities. Barbara Walters is brilliant and scintillating —and as a result sometimes outshines the people she interviews. Studs Terkel projects an infectious excitement. The late Frank McGee was invariably friendly, interested, and low-key; it all added up to *sincerity.* Robert Cromie (*Book Beat,* Public Broadcast) is relaxed and personable and well-prepared: he often knows the book better than the author. Jeanne Wolf (*Jeanne Wolf With . . . ,* Public Broadcast) puts a high degree of conversational intensity into her thirty-minute interviews, which she describes as a "pressure cooker" situation. "I can ask questions that would take three months to get to in normal conversations," she explained in a newspaper interview. "You can cut past the small talk. . . . It's simply people chemistry. I don't have to do any commercials so we can have a half-hour of solid build. We can get very intense and very personal when it's not interrupted."

THE QUICKIE INTERVIEW

The most common broadcast interview is the "quickie," the kind you see daily on the evening news: a thirty-second taped or filmed commentary—or "actuality" as broadcasters call it—extracted from a brief conversation. Broadcast interviewers don't waste time. They try to get right to the point of any situation. The typical quickie interview consists of a few minutes of pretaping conversation out of which the reporter grasps the nature of the story and phrases two or three "quick questions" designed to elicit two or three equally quick answers. The camera rolls, the Q's and A's spill out, the camera shuts down, and the interviewer is off to another assignment.

Clearly problems exist in this kind of interview, which is common in local radio and television stations. Professor Karl Nestvold, who teaches broadcast news courses at the University of Oregon, outlines the problems in six categories.

1. Poorly informed interviewer. The broadcast reporter is spread so thin that he has little time for preparation. He's under constant deadline pressure.

2. Extremely short interviews. Not much time for creative exchange of ideas.

3. Frequent need for summing up complex issues in thirty seconds. This produces simplistic commentary.

4. Anxiety about equipment failure. "If it's not airable, the greatest interview in the world is no good."

5. The frequently successful effort by public figures to control the interview. Because there's time for only a couple of questions, the respondent makes sure he gives the answers he wants to give, no matter what the questions.

6. Fear by respondents that tape or film clips will be excerpted and played out of context, changing the intended meaning. This dampens interviews with wary sources.

Perhaps another problem of the broadcast quickie is the practice of thrusting the microphone back and forth between questioner and respondent. It seems somehow reminiscent of the flashing swordplay of Douglas Fairbanks, Jr. In her research paper, Margaret Laine took special note of an interesting TV interview with Idaho Senator Frank Church.

> At the start of the interview, the interviewer held the mike a comfortable distance from the senator. When she asked a question that Church evaded, she thrust the microphone closer. As the interview

progressed, the interviewer continued to shove the mike more and more-hostilely toward the senator's face. By the end of the interview the senator had begun to rock back on his heels to escape the microphone's spear-like thrust. Finally he actually stepped back from the interviewer—who immediately stepped forward. . . . Interestingly, both interviewer and interviewee exchanged smiles at the close of the interview, seemingly totally oblivious of the microphone dynamics I had observed.

The mike might better be kept stationary between the two. Some reporters prefer to have the respondent hold it. Lavaliere mikes, which hang around the neck like a pendant, are another solution.

Laine concludes:

What does it take to be a broadcast interviewer? In addition to being more human than a computer and more articulate than a chimpanzee, a broadcast interviewer should be: perceptive, intelligent, curious, warm, persistent, imaginative, flexible, creative, responsive, resourceful, sincere, tough, sympathetic, alert, brave, and self-confident. . . . The good broadcast interviewer conducts interviews that produce new information for the audience, for the interviewee, and for himself. With skillful questions, he puts old facts together in a new way that may cause even the most hardened and cynical political figure to express a new opinion or come up with a new idea or simply be spontaneous and frank.

THE SPIRIT OF BROADCAST INTERVIEWING

If it seems hopelessly impossible, remember that good broadcast interviewing is one of the most demanding journalistic endeavors. It is not merely a matter of getting information. It is, rather, a *performance*. It is an intense conversation that draws on the rich interplay of two minds, at least one of which is conscious of the needs and interests of an unseen audience. When well done the conversation seems to draw energy from its own interpersonal dynamics.

The analogy with floating down the roaring river—exciting rapids interspersed with deep pools, with one never quite knowing what's around the next bend—is apt. The rapids represent a rapid by-play of conversation between the two participants. The deep pools represent the thoughtful conceptual statements certain to emerge from good talk. A well-paced interview includes both. It also has that extra quality of moving forward on a strong conversational current toward the exciting possibility of new discovery. Like an explorer you push forward, hoping for some heretofore unseen vista to unfold—a new insight into the character of your guest, a fresh view on some current political or social or economic issue, or

"THIS CONCLUDES OUR INTERVIEW FROM THE LOCKER
ROOM. NOW WE KNOW HOW A LOSING COACH FEELS!"

Rothco

perhaps a graphic demonstration of a strongly held belief (for example, a beauty queen gets rightfully indignant at public curiosity about her romantic life).

The interviewer must never lose track of his special role in broadcasting: it is *more* than processing information. To fill the role properly, the interviewer must be especially well prepared. It is the *interviewer's* knowledge and perception and creative imagination that shape and guide the interview and suggest what topics to bring up, what questions to ask, and how to react to or follow up on the answers. If a broadcaster were to interview the police chief on employment of women as patrol officers, for example, he might follow the lead of the article writer and conduct preinterview discussions with some of the women themselves. Suppose then that the chief says on the air that the department treats men and women precisely the same. You respond that you've interviewed several of the women and you've read several books and reports, all suggesting that men and women are *not* the same and that some accommodation has to be made in departmental policy for the difference. You'll get a better answer, you can be sure, as a result of that input or "exchange" of information. He may not agree with your conclusion. He may even convince you and/or the audience that it's wrong. But he'll give you sharper, more precise answers as a result of your comment. At least he'll realize he can't snow you. You've done your homework.

You've also become terribly *involved* in the conversation—perhaps, like Studs Terkel, even excited. You're exhilarated and so is the respondent. You're on your toes, asking questions with an extra sense of urgency. You're smiling, even laughing, and the atmosphere is, well . . . electric.

The best interviews are those where you forget the setting, the cameras and all, and you become immersed in the conversation and all its subtle points. You almost (but not quite!) become so engrossed as to ignore the floor director who is frantically trying to get you to notice the thirty-second time cue. *Only thirty seconds left!* How could the time have gone so fast?

NINE

The Personality Interview

Q. Professor, I want to ask your views about older students coming back to college. Frankly, I'm getting nothing but runarounds from the faculty. I realize the college needs more students, but I didn't think *all* the professors would be so public relations conscious. Well, what do *you* think about older students?

A. Ah, I suppose they're not much different from other students—some good, some lousy—

Q. That's what they *all* say! I just don't understand why nobody will give me anything startling or different!

Personalities have always fascinated Americans, perhaps even more than issues or events. At this writing the world still awaits the "real" story of Patricia Hearst—not just the superficial reports of her court trials, but the *inside* story: the one that crawls inside her mind and reveals the personal motivations, desires, frustrations, fantasies, and experiences that help to explain why the overindulged and bored rich girl became the nation's most celebrated kidnap victim. Unraveling the Patty Hearst mystery should keep a battery of biographers busy for years.

Most biographical articles, except those done about persons long dead, involve interviews. In the strictest sense, of course, all interviews except those done by computer are "personality" interviews. Any interaction between two human beings can never be devoid of the human element. The recurring problem of survey research interviewing is that of trying to minimize personality to eliminate personal bias in the statistical result. The journalistic personality interview is roughly the opposite. The interaction between the two personalities produces a higher level of "intelligence" than either person could produce alone. The interviewer is working to draw out the respondent; he in turn is "performing." The resultant article often shows a personality more lively and interesting than his friends and family ever knew him to be. That's because a skilled interviewer has asked questions and obtained answers no one else thought of considering. It may also be because the respondent has truly been *listened* to for the first time in years.

In a superficial sense the personality interview is among the easiest to do. Most people enjoy talking about themselves to anyone who will listen. Often they are remarkably candid about the intimate details of their private lives, a fact that unnerves many novice interviewers. They don't know how to respond to such personal details, and so they hasten to safe ground with resultant damage to interviewing rapport. A business executive wants to talk about her unhappy childhood as a means of explaining her relentless pursuit of achievement, but the interviewer quashes it all by insensitively changing the subject: "Tell me what you do with your leisure time."

Columnist Rex Reed has found the candor of show business celebrities simply astounding. He told John Brady of *Writer's Digest:* "It's incredible when you stop to think about the number of very famous people who have really treated me like an analyst. All they've done is save themselves $60 an hour, but they've told me all their problems."

Other interviewers, however, consider celebrities hopelessly predictable in their answers. Studs Terkel, in the introduction to his best-selling *Working,* discusses the use of his primary interviewing tool, the tape recorder.

> It can be used to capture the voice of a celebrity, whose answers are ever ready and flow through all the expected straits. I have yet to be astonished by one. It can be used to capture the thoughts of the non-celebrated—on the steps of a public housing project, in a frame bungalow, in a furnished apartment, in a parked car—and these "statistics" become persons, each one unique. I am constantly astonished.

The problem with celebrity interviews is what one writer calls "self-creation." Celebrities have built such complicated façades for their public images that they are incapable of being, or even *finding,* themselves. Explains Thomas B. Morgan in the introduction to his book, *Self-Creations: 13 Impersonalities:* "Most better-known people tend toward an elegant solution of what they, or their advisers, call 'the image problem.' Over time, deliberately, they create a public self for the likes of me to interview, observe, and double-check."

Morgan describes the archetype as Brigitte Bardot: "The existential focus of her self-creation was the exercise of power over men." She proceeded to demonstrate that power by inviting (through her husband) Morgan to come to France to interview her. She broke an appointment and kept him waiting for a week before she suddenly and precipitously agreed to an interview.

Maurice Zolotow, who has written personality articles and biographies about show business personalities, concludes that "the problem· of the profile writer becomes a problem in understanding the characters of his subjects and in grasping the roots of their present patterns of behavior. The problem, in other words, is psychological" *(Writer's Digest Handbook of Article Writing)*.

The complexities of writing about people are perhaps best summarized by the late French novelist and biographer, André Maurois: "Except in those rare cases in which [the biographer] is writing the history of a man whose life happens to have constructed itself, he is obliged to take over a shapeless mass, made up of unequal fragments and prolonged in every direction by isolated groups of events which lead nowhere" (Whitman, *The Obituary Book*).

Such comments suggest that the personality interview is at once the simplest yet most complex and frustrating of journalistic endeavors. And it's probably the most fascinating, at least for those who enjoy people.

That's the key—enjoying people. Being curious about them. Wondering what they're *really* like and how they got that way. You don't necessarily have to *like* all of them. But you must appreciate them for their ability to tell you things you didn't already know. Even the most despicable of characters can be interesting in a perverse sense as, for example, the two killers in Truman Capote's *In Cold Blood*. Nobody said an interviewer must agree with the actions of his respondents. You are there to *listen,* not to judge. You are also there to discover, if you can, the good that exists in the worst of people and the bad in the best.

Of course various levels of the personality interview exist. It's not as though you're going to write a book-length biography of a glamorous film star tomorrow. The best way to start with personality interviewing is to start first with simple interviews and then more complex ones as you gain experience.

USES OF PERSONALITY INTERVIEWS

Whatever the complexities of the personality interview, there should remain no doubt of its importance. People like to read about people. A dramatic indication of growing public interest in personalities is the singular success in a period of economic recession of the new magazine established by Time, Inc. in 1974: *People*. In just eighteen months *People* was in the black financially with spectacular gains in circulation and advertising. Its success has spawned several imitators, such as *In the Know*, *Celebrity*, and *Faces*. "This is a magazine devoted entirely to people," says Dick Stolley, editor of *People*. "We don't deal with issues; we don't deal with events; we don't deal with debate. We deal *only* with human beings."

The magazine's success under such a philosophy bodes well for the future of the personality interview. You need not look far, however, to discover similar changes in other media. Since the 1950s newspapers have experimented with "humanistic" reporting, depicting people in various news situations or seeing events through the subjective eyes of one observer. *Time* and *Newsweek* have been doing that for years. Nonfiction writers have long known that personality adds spirit to otherwise lifeless articles about issues or trends.

Another demonstration of the trend is the change taking place in what used to be the newspaper society, culture, and women's sections. They are being replaced by sections with names like "Style," "Today," "People," and "Living." The big pictures of brides are being replaced by interviews with race track drivers, incorrigible teenage girls, tugboat captains, coal miners, and loggers. The old society page is clearly not the same any more. Replacing it are articles representing some of the most creative personality interviewing in the newspaper.

Finally, it's noteworthy that various kinds of comprehensive personality nonfiction are becoming attractive to persons with literary names, such as Truman Capote who, upon release of his nonfiction novel, *In Cold Blood*, called "reportage" the great "unexplored art form of the future." No longer is the novel the only vehicle for the study of human character. One observer, Tom Wolfe, author of *The Electric Kool-Aid Acid Test*, suggests that the nonfiction novel is replacing the Great American Novel. John Fischer, former editor of *Harper's*, has called the nonfiction article the "characteristic literary medium of our generation," as was the epic poem of ancient Greece or the poetic drama of Elizabethan England. He adds, "The novelists who are most widely read, who earn the most, and who have the heaviest impact on public opinion are now usually the so-called 'nonfiction novelists.' These are writers who choose a public theme —war, the uses of power, the moral dilemmas of our society—as contrasted with the 'literary' novelists who prefer to deal with purely private emotions: the miseries of drug addicts and homosexuals are two momentary favorites."

Fischer made those remarks in 1963, several years before the term "new journalism" came into general use in the late 1960s. The most enduring definition of new journalism suggests neither advocacy nor underground journalism but rather a brand of "people" journalism: the use of the techniques of the fiction writer in nonfiction works, including plot, characterization, scenes, dialogue, description, and point of view. This becomes "people" journalism simply because it is difficult to have dialogue, characterization, plot, point of view, etc., without putting people on your pages.

This puts heretofore unheard-of demands on the interview because the scenes and dialogue cannot come from imagination. Mostly they come from intense research, participant-observation, and interviewing. Tom Wolfe explained in a September 1970 article in the ASNE *Bulletin* that the new journalism depends largely on "saturation reporting":

> You are after not just facts. The basic units of reporting are no longer who-what-where-how and why but whole scenes and stretches of dialogue. The New Journalism involves a depth of reporting and an attention to the most minute facts and details that most news-papermen, even the most experienced, have never dreamed of. To pull it off you casually have to stay with the people you are writing about for long stretches. You may have to stay with them for days, weeks, even months—long enough so that you are actually there when revealing scenes take place in their lives. You have to con-stantly be on the alert for chance remarks, odd details, quirks, curios, anything that may serve to bring a scene alive when you're writing. There is no formula for it.

You might assume that such intensity of reporting must necessarily be limited to the writers of magazine articles and nonfiction books. Though clearly book-length nonfiction offers more maneuvering room to develop plot and characterization, the newspaper series offers similar opportunities to any journalist willing to take the time and trouble. An excellent example is the work of Lucinda Franks and Thomas Powers, of United Press International, about Diana Oughton, an underground revolutionary killed in a New York City bomb factory explosion in 1970. The story, which Powers later expanded into a book, traces the slow transformation of this upper middle-class girl into a member of the violently radical Weathermen underground.

TYPES OF PERSONALITY ARTICLES

Do not assume that interviews come in two distinct classes—personality and nonpersonality, that is, people on the one hand and issues and events on the other. The best articles combine the two, showing people intensely involved with issues. General topics such as poverty or hunger are too abstract for most people's tastes. But to talk about one family's poverty or what one crusading person is doing to solve the hunger problem is dramatic and concrete.

To better understand the various ways in which the human element fits into journalistic interviews, let's examine some common types of "people" stories, ranging from the simplest to the most complex.

The Personal Sidelight

This is the inclusion of a human dimension to a more or less routine article. When *Newsweek* wrote recently about "The Trucker Mystique" (January 26, 1976) it led into the subject by talking about *one* truck driver: "It is 11 P.M. when Ben Rosson brakes his eighteen-wheeler and turns into the Union 76 truck stop in Ontario, Calif. . . ."

By the same concept, a routine news story about an automobile accident becomes nonroutine once the human dimension is understood. Let's say the car plummeted over a bank into a raging, rain-swollen river. A young woman passing by the scene jumped into the icy water and swam twenty yards to rescue two children trapped inside the half-submerged vehicle. The story is no longer routine; it is, by some standards of news judgment, a bigger story than if the children had died. Why? Because it lends itself to dramatic personal narrative. Who is this young woman? Why did she choose to risk her life? How does she feel about her act of heroism in retrospect? People are curious about such things. They'll read an article that presents the answers.

Another type of personal sidelight is the use of specific testimony to buttress a point. One newspaper's account of the increase of long-distance travel by bus contained a wealth of facts and figures. But the heart of the story was "why?"—why the growing use of buses? The answer was effectively presented by the quoted testimony of the bus riders themselves: the young musician enroute from Chicago to Nashville with more time than money, the young woman with two children enroute to meet her husband at a military base, the elderly couple enjoying a tour.

The Personality Sidebar

This is a separate story that a newspaper or magazine runs in conjunction with a general story on an issue or event. The account of a disastrous flood is supplemented by a more personal account of one family's experience.

U.S. News ran an article on runaway wives (February 23, 1976) and incorporated into the two-page report a separate account of one woman's experience. It described her unhappy marriage (made worse by discovering her husband's extramarital affairs), her sudden decision to run away (she planned it while lying awake beside her husband, and she left the very next morning), and her restrospective feelings about it ("I resent being judged. . . . I can see it in people's eyes. They're wondering what kind of woman I am. . . .").

The main purpose of the sidebar is to provide a personal dimension to an issue or event. Such articles are usually short and pointed. They usually include a narrative account of what happened to that person and why, along with an explanation of how the person feels about it in retrospect.

The Personality Sketch

The sketch is brief, to the point, and usually covers a narrow range of topics, sometimes only one. Rather than being a full-blown personality story about the mayor, the sketch centers on one event: his role in getting the city council to approve the building of a new fire station. The sketch comes in two dimensions, the narrative and the backgrounder.

Narrative. This is roughly the same as the sidebar, described above, except that it stands alone. It's usually the account of some person's involvement in a situation and how that person views the situation now. Most of the articles in *People* and its imitators fall into this category. They are short, pointed, lively accounts related to the person's rise to (or decline from) prominence: He's recently written a best-selling novel. . . . she's assumed management of her late father's far-flung corporate enterprise. . . . he's living a serene life now after his misadventures of a year or two ago. . . . she's an up-and-coming personality about which the world will hear much in the months ahead. . . . and so forth.

Backgrounder. This differs from the narrative in that it is usually a brief compendium of background details about a person deemed worthy of attention. Newspapers run these regularly as "personalities behind the news." Let's say the city police department has appointed a new chief of detectives. The backgrounder runs a day or two after the first announcement and contains a variety of details related to that person's new job: his previous work, his philosophy of law enforcement, his views of problems and trends.

The Feature Interview

The feature interview is an article based on one or more interviews with the subject of the story. It is by far the most common kind of personality article, particularly in newspapers. A celebrity comes to town—the secretary of health, education and welfare, we'll say—and a news reporter interviews him in a wide-ranging conversation that covers everything from Washington politics to shrinking funds for social science research. The writer may incorporate some descriptive material or biographical data.

Other examples include such things as an interview with the governor on the "state of the state," an interview with the governor's wife about her volunteer work, an interview with a woman who builds racy little aerobatic airplanes in her garage and flies them in air shows. Such articles come in two basic categories, thematic and nonthematic.

The nonthematic interview.   This is the most common, particularly in newspapers. The Q–A format (such as *Playboy*'s) falls into this category, as do some other magazine interviews such as the series of interviews, "Pete Martin Calls On . . ." that ran in the *Saturday Evening Post* in the late 1950s and 1960s.

In a more recent example, actress Sophia Loren discusses a variety of topics ("The Truth about Sophia," by Alan Levy, *McCall's*, September 1975). She denies that her marriage is shaky; she relives the time she was accosted by an armed robber in a New York hotel; she expresses her views on such topics as American women ("Some . . . are too masculine sometimes").

The thematic interview.   This confines itself to a specific topic or a set of closely related topics. A celebrity interview does not cover all possible topics but confines itself to her latest movie or book, or his marriage, or her views on feminism, or his experiences in combating alcoholism. In one recent interview (by Vernon Scott, *Ladies' Home Journal*, September 1975), Mary Tyler Moore and her husband, Grant Tinker, discuss only one thing: their separation and subsequent reconciliation. The advantage of the thematic interview is the greater detail it provides on one topic in contrast to the superficial glance at many topics in the nonthematic interview.

Thematic or nonthematic, the distinguishing characteristic of the feature interview is that it's essentially a record of the comments of the respondent. The interviewer's job is to record faithfully what that person says about the topic or topics brought up for discussion. Although the article may appear in first person ("I asked Marilyn this question . . ."), the interviewer does not attempt to make major subjective judgments about the person, nor does he consider himself a participant in the life of the person.

Many interviews are done on a catch-as-catch-can basis; the visiting celebrity may or may not be willing to talk. A newspaper interview with Katharine Hepburn visiting Oregon (by Ted Mahar, *The Oregonian*, October 4, 1974) ranged from discussions of leading men to getting "up" emotionally for scenes. But the largest portion of it was, interestingly, about why she almost never grants interviews:

> I don't like to give interviews. I worry about being sufficiently interesting for one thing. I mean, an interview is a performance of a sort,

isn't it? If I'm working very hard on the set—and I do work very hard—it's very difficult for me to come down from the intensity of the mood and try to tell someone how wonderful I am and then resume the emotion of the scene.

The Case History

For years the *Ladies' Home Journal* has run one of its most enduring and popular features, one entitled "Can This Marriage Be Saved?" The format is standard. First one anonymous partner to an estranged marriage gives a version of the problem; then the other partner gives a version. Finally a counselor provides a summarizing kind of insight and relates what eventually happened to the marriage. The key to success of this feature is the candid detail—sufficient detail so that the readers can identify with the problem, perhaps even learn something about their own marriages. It's a perfect example of a kind of personality interview known as the case history.

The case history is dramatic and readable primarily because it *shows* in detail the personality through the actions described. It can be adapted to a variety of situations ranging from marital relationships to executive decision making. Case histories come in two basic types, the sidelight and the stand-alone.

The sidelight. This is a longer version of the personality sidebar described earlier. In the longer lengths it is most commonly seen in books. You're writing a book, say, on executive stress. You've interviewed hundreds of business executives and government bureaucrats about their sleepless nights, their drinking, their marital troubles—fallout from their tension-filled jobs. Your interview with one of them is more dramatic, detailed, and insightful than the others, so you devote an entire chapter to his case history: "The story of John Doe, executive vice president for production."

The stand-alone. This version, common to magazine and newspaper articles, looks at a subject through one major and detailed example. You're writing about the problems, say, of adopting mixed-race orphans. You do it by depicting the experiences of one couple who adopted several of them. Into the story of the "Smith family," you weave general information about the subject to give it a national perspective. You may even include examples from other families, but the major focus is on the Smith family.

At its best the case history reads like an intimate diary, showing not only what the subject said and did but also what he thought. You show your executive making a difficult decision that may affect the lives of hundreds of workers. What factors did he consider in the decision? How did he weigh the pros and cons? Whom did he consult? What did these consultants tell him? What was said in conferences? What did he tell his family and friends? How well did he sleep? How much did he drink? Did he take tranquilizers? What was his general mood during the process of decision? What *was* his decision, and what has happened as a result?

Two major difficulties beset the case history. One is the need for intimate detail—the kind of material that can be obtained only from interviews because none of it ever gets into official documents. This means interviewing for detail, getting respondents to recall minute events of the past. This is hard. It isn't made easier by the fact that you may have to cope with several versions of the same conversation as you interview different participants. The final test is this question: Have you given the reader sufficient detail that he could reasonably add up the factors himself and come out with a decision different from the one made by your executive? If not, then go back for more detail.

The second problem is one of confidentiality. If you are going to identify the person, you may not be able to publish all the private thoughts or intimate detail for fear of damaging his reputation or invading his privacy. Running the material anonymously weakens it; you also run the risk that the details themselves are sufficient to permit easy identification. In national publication, the problem is less severe. Some literary license is commonly exercised in changing details sufficiently to avoid identification—a fact that you should point out in the article. Some writers use "composites": the "person" characterized is actually a combination of several persons interviewed.

In one famous case a New York writer described the activities of a prostitute named Redpants in amazing detail. The one detail omitted was that Redpants wasn't real; she was a composite of several hustlers the writer had interviewed. But Redpants wasn't *not* real, either, since she was based on real persons. The composite nature of Redpants was not mentioned in the article, though the editor of *New York,* the magazine that carried the article, said his staff would be more careful in the future about alerting readers whenever a composite is used.

The Profile

The *New Yorker* pioneered the profile in the late 1920s. Its writers, not content merely to record the words of a celebrity, elected to write personality portrayals based on extensive research, including wide-ranging interviews of the persons closest to the subject: friends, enemies, business associates, family, servants—anyone who could add insight or anecdotal detail. The result was not only more comprehensive but it included the dark side of the person's character, thus delivering a more honest, realistic, and believable portrait. With so many diverse views of the subject, the writer is bound to uncover all the hidden nuances of a personality. He can therefore write more candidly under the guiding philosophy of André Malraux, who once said that the truth about a man lies first and foremost in what he hides.

Most profiles contain, overtly or implicitly, a thematic statement, a notion of a central characteristic about that person. She's spurred on by ruthless ambition. . . . he's so insecure that he must dominate the lives of those around him. . . . publicly she's a happy-go-lucky clown but privately she's a melancholy person. . . . and so forth. Admittedly, such themes tend to be simplistic, particularly at the hands of an inexperienced or overzealous writer. Sometimes the writer simply shows his person in action, leaving the conclusions to be drawn by the reader. Even so, the writer cannot avoid making subjective judgments in his selection of material to include.

The profile places heavy demands on interviewing ability, particularly for writers who portray the personality through anecdotes, scenes, and dialogue. This includes all good personality profile writers because the only way to make a person come alive on paper is to *show* him in action. Some writers, of course, are better at showing action than others are.

Profiles come in three basic categories.

Objective. The writer is a detached observer who does not attempt to enter into the activities or become part of the subject's life. The news magazine cover story is an excellent example: a portrayal of a person through the essentials of good journalistic research, including interviews with the subject and persons surrounding the subject. The objective profile usually follows a standard pattern of writing. It starts with an anecdotal narrative leading to a general statement of theme—something like "at thirty-four the young executive has parlayed a $1,000 initial investment and an uncanny talent for shrewd real estate dealing into a multimillion-dollar business. . . ." The article then proceeds through quotes and incidents to trace and explain the young executive's rise to prominence.

Participant-observer. The writer abandons his detached mode of operation and becomes a participant with the subject, though not necessarily a full-fledged one. The writer will stay with the subject for long stretches, days, weeks, even years in one celebrated case that produced the book, *Honor Thy Father,* by Gay Talese, a portrayal of a Mafia gangster, Bill Bonanno. Though Talese spent much time with the Mafia, clearly he was not part of it. He says of the experience (Associated Press interview, 1971):

> I tried to use a more imaginative approach to reporting. I never quote directly, never use a tape recorder. I'm interested in what a

person thinks, not what he said, because often what a person says is not what he really believes.

Because I was able to spend so much time with the family, I learned their attitudes. If I took notes, it was only to re-establish my role as a reporter. I was very close to Bill, but I was still an outsider. I took my notebook out occasionally just to remind him why I was there.

When the writer is there, the primary task is to be alert for the truly revealing scenes to take place. He must recognize them when he sees them. He cannot do that, Talese once said, unless vast preliminary research and interviewing have preceded it. That's the only way to *know* whether a happening is truly revealing or not.

Single-incident narrative. This combines several other categories, including the case history. What distinguishes it from the others is that you choose to portray a character through a single incident or sequence of incidents in his life, often by being there when they take place. Suppose you are writing about an important business executive who enjoys mountain climbing. You accompany him on one of his climbs, and you describe his activities, his conversations, and his relationships with others in graphic detail. Perhaps analogies are possible. The climb becomes symbolic: he attacks mountains in the same way he attacks business problems. He feels the same exhilaration upon reaching the top. Your best "interview" may come at the top. A mountain climber once told me that in the chill, breathless atmosphere of a mountaintop, a lot of truths get expressed that don't come out in the guarded atmosphere of the executive suite.

A famous example of the single-incident narrative is Lillian Ross's portrayal of the late Ernest Hemingway on a two-day visit to New York. She spent much time with him, and her account of his activities not only reads like a short story, complete with plot, but it creates so vivid and lively a portrayal of Hemingway that a lot of his fans became unnerved. The article was highly controversial, though Hemingway himself is said to have liked it. (See this and other examples of Ross's nonfiction narrative work in her book *Reporting.* Among them is the book *Picture,* a narrative account of the filming of John Huston's *Red Badge of Courage.* Some observers credit *Picture* as the prototype of the "nonfiction novel"; it came out in 1952, thirteen years before Capote's *In Cold Blood.*)

INTERVIEWING TECHNIQUES

If the personality interview were seeking only the routine facts of a person's life—date of birth, college degrees, career changes, number of mountains climbed (actually or symbolically)—it would be simple indeed.

But for the full-blown personality story you are seeking, in addition to routine facts, two basic aspects of the person. Neither is simple in terms of interviewing technique.

First you want to understand what that person is like. Where did he come from, where is he now, how did he get there, and where is he headed? What factors have influenced his life? This aspect would be simple enough if there were any concrete answers. Usually there are not. A person simply lives his life, a life composed of thousands of odd-shaped fragments like jigsaw puzzle pieces. They defy any artistic-journalistic endeavor to piece them together. Often—I'm tempted to say *usually*—the respondent can offer very little help in understanding the overall concepts of his life. He is as confused as everybody else. Sometimes you may be the first person to inquire of such things. You then become involved in an interchange of ideas that may lead to some joint conclusions about the meaning of his life. Or they may lead nowhere in particular. This is particularly true of celebrities. It is difficult, sometimes impossible, to penetrate the exterior image they have created for themselves, and so you are left to describe the orange peelings instead of the orange.

The second basic aspect of the personality interview is the assembling of specific illustrative data to support, clarify, and dramatize the basic concepts if and when you come to understand them. This means *showing* the personality through anecdotes and scenes and dialogue, many of which are gained through personal observation. The hardest part of this is recognizing a scene or snippet of conversation as being important.

Things happen. Art—even the journalistic art of the personality story —is "created" or at least "rendered."

The inexperienced writer often has trouble perceiving the significance of everyday events. To the alert writer, however, even the most commonplace of scenes can have meaning. Biographer Maurice Zolotow once traveled by train with Jack Benny, and it was in the process of dining with him that he discovered a revealing characteristic: "how uneasy and lacking in confidence Mr. Benny is in his real character. He never knew what to order. . . . He'd say, 'What are you ordering?' or, pointing to an adjoining table, 'What's that they are eating over there? Looks good.' "

Such scenes are often overlooked. A man comes off a plane in Los Angeles and is greeted by his wife at the airport. She starts to kiss him, then stops short. She asks what became of his necktie.

Big deal. Pretty ordinary stuff.

Yet in the hands of a skilled writer like Gay Talese, even so ordinary a scene becomes part of a creative art—the art of the personality story. Not only did Talese start out an *Esquire* article with just such an incident, but another writer, Tom Wolfe, singled out that article as representing "the first time I realized there was something new going on in journalism." With such a testimonial, the incident deserves a careful examination. The article depicted Joe Louis at age fifty and it started out with a scene between Louis and his third wife.

> "Hi, Sweetheart!" Joe Louis called to his wife, spotting her waiting for him at the Los Angeles airport.
> She smiled, walked toward him, and was about to stretch up on her toes and kiss him—but suddenly stopped.
> "Joe," she snapped, "where's your tie?"
> "Aw, sweetie," Joe Louis said, shrugging, "I stayed out all night in New York and didn't have time."
> "All night!" she cut in. "When you're out here with me all you do is sleep, sleep, sleep."
> "Sweetie," Joe Louis said, with a tired grin, "I'm an ole man."
> "Yes," she agreed, "but when you go to New York you try to be young again."

Talese had witnessed the incident. No lightning struck at the time; no shafts of light fell upon the scene to tell the writer that this was a significant scene. Talese merely recognized its significance as part of a portrait of Joe Louis at fifty, and he recorded it in his article. A less perceptive writer might well have ignored it.

Some Special Interviewing Approaches

The techniques for personality interviews are not unlike those of any other interview, just more so. The purpose must be more specific and more clearly stated to the respondent, even if it's "to learn everything I can about you so that I can write an article that *shows*—not just tells— what you're really like." The advance preparation must be more complete, the rapport must be better, the questions more perceptive, the listening more sensitive. And the *bomb* . . . the bomb may be ever more explosive, but it must be ever-more-gently lowered into the conversation.

Mostly it's a matter of being interested. Caring. Listening. "I got people to talk," said Gay Talese of his intimate interviews for a new book on the sexual revolution, "because I care and I'm interested."

Listening must contain more than empathy, however; it must contain perception. The most productive kind of listening is akin to that of the psychoanalyst hearing out a patient. In that context, the words of the late Theodor Reik *(Listening with the Third Ear)* are instructive.

> The analyst hears not only what is in the words; he hears also what the words do not say. He listens with the "third ear," hearing not only what the patient speaks but also his own inner voices, what emerges from his own unconscious depths. Mahler once remarked, "The most important thing in music is not the score." In psychoanalysis, too, what is spoken is not the most important thing. It

appears to us more important to recognize what speech conceals and what silence reveals.[1]

Catherine Drinker Bowen has further advice in her *Adventures of a Biographer:*

> An interviewer, I have sometimes thought, is like a woman invited to waltz to music; she must follow easily, no matter how intricate the side steps. A little tactful steering can put the conversation back on track, but there is no room for forcing or impatience.

Questions in the personality interview may range from the abstract to the concrete, from serious to humorous, from philosophical to anecdotal —even from sublime to ridiculous. A ridiculous question will often elicit a ridiculous answer. But that answer may reveal an offbeat, idiosyncratic aspect of a personality. Someone asked an elegantly gowned Miss America contestant if she wouldn't be just as happy lounging around in her old, faded, patched-up blue jeans, and she replied, "My heavens, yes!" She said it was her mother who had gotten her into this mess; she didn't enjoy it. As Miss Oregon she'd made no fewer than two hundred personal appearances all over the state—a killing pace. She said the pageant exploited the good nature of young women. And that was before the days of feminism. So a "ridiculous" question opened up a whole new interviewing vista and gave an interesting perception not only of the young woman but of the whole idea of beauty contests.

But perhaps the heart of creative personality interviewing is the perception the interviewer brings into the conversation. He sees things that others don't see. That's because he listens carefully and he's forever trying to put two and two together. Let's say you're interviewing a film star. Her almost imperceptibly raised eyebrow at one point plus a big smile at another plus animated discussion of topics like parachuting and mountain climbing plus accounts of several narrow escapes total up to a conclusion that she's never happier than when confronted by physical danger. She loves avalanches, mountain blizzards, and tangled parachute lines. To this you may add other points gained from sources outside the interview. Ultimately you develop a creative hypothesis to try out on her: "Miss Jones, you seem to have a strong need for physical adventure, possibly even misadventure. You remind me a little of Winston Churchill who said during World War II, 'Nothing is so exhilarating as to be shot at without effect.' What do you think of that?" And she says, "Maybe that's so." She's never thought of it before. She merely does what she does and is what she is. It's up to her "biographer" to make interpretations and bring some order to these fragments.

---

[1] Theodor Reik, *Listening with the Third Ear.* © 1952 by Farrar, Straus & Giroux, Inc. Reprinted by permission of the publisher.

The personality interviewer also learns to look for the hidden dimensions of seemingly ordinary things. Tom Wolfe once remarked in a radio interview that in reporting crime newspapers invariably select certain details for publication. Mostly they are loss of property, loss of life, and injuries. That's what they consider reality. But Wolfe says the "reality of a criminal act is *terror*—terror on the part of both the assailant and the victim." He has a point. If you begin asking questions about the emotional aspects of crime—the terror, the anguish, the humiliation—you open up a new vista of creative interviewing.

This is particularly important for the personality interview. You must explore the hidden dimensions and you must make it possible for the respondent to say what he *really thinks or feels*. It takes an element of objectivity. You're making it possible, say, for a woman to say how she really feels about the terror, frustration, and humiliation of being attacked on a dark street at night, but you're not passing personal judgment on, say, the fact that she chose to submit to the rape rather than risk being hurt or killed.

Some Problems of Saturation Reporting

Darlene Ingle, a graduate student at the University of Oregon in 1973, researched the interviewing techniques of three writers, Tom Wolfe, Truman Capote, and Gay Talese. She found three recurring themes in their methods of "saturation reporting" that make their brand of new journalism different from traditional interviewing.

1. Time. It takes longer. "Even though in-depth interviewing takes a much greater amount of time . . . it may work to the interviewer's advantage. Most people are flattered by attention if approached correctly. With more time at his disposal, the interviewer has a better opportunity to establish good rapport."

2. An easy-going relationship in which the interviewer maintains a low-profile, unobtrusive manner. He "need not bombard his subject with questions. Most people are more responsive if allowed to discuss subjects which interest them at their leisure."

3. An approach that considers *everything* as potentially important. "Being aware of detail means noting everything that applies to the subject's life: his everyday habits, gestures, manners, customs, household surroundings, styles of traveling, eating, keeping house, expressions, manner of walking, and the thousands of little peculiarities that go into the makeup of an individual. Sensual information, color, tastes, smell, sounds, and tactile impressions are all important."

Ingle also interviewed a member of novelist Ken Kesey's Merry Pranksters, subject of Tom Wolfe's book, *The Electric Kool-Aid Acid Test*.

"Wolfe was really fantastic," said Ken Babbs. "He never took notes, just hung around, and then went home at night and wrote the whole thing up." [2]

Personality Interviewing Questions

Most interviewers have favorite methods, special questions, for getting their subjects to speak candidly about themselves. Studs Terkel likes to ask, "When did the window open?" as a means of starting a respondent off on a philosophical discussion of how he came to hold a certain set of beliefs. "Was there any one time, was there one teacher, one influence, or was it an accretion of events?" (See Brian, *Murderers and Other Friendly People*, 1973.)

Though mindful that the personality interview is a complex human relationship that defies a simple set of questions, I nonetheless present the following list of possible avenues of inquiry. It is distilled from interviews with many journalists and from reading about the methods of writers from Francis Bacon through James Boswell to Truman Capote.

1. What contrivances, material things, does the respondent surround himself with? Cars, clothes, the house he lives in, mementos? How about "toys" such as tape recorders, trophies, cameras, stereos, scrapbooks?

2. What does he read? Books, magazines, special newspapers? What's on his living room bookshelf or coffee table (in contrast to what he reads in the privacy of his bedroom)?

3. Who are his heroes, political, historical, literary, theatrical?

4. What kinds of people does he surround himself with? What's his spouse like? His friends? His subordinates?

5. What are his goals in life, professionally and personally, short- and long-range? How's he doing toward reaching them? What stands in his way?

6. What are his major problems, professionally and personally? What's he doing about them?

7. How does he spend his leisure time? Where does he take his vacations? With whom? What does he do?

8. What is a typical day on the job like for him?

9. What kinds of issues, concepts, philosophies, etc., really matter to him, both professionally and personally? When and how did he first become aware of them? What actions has he taken (or will he take) in support of them?

2 Darlene Ingle, "Interviewing and the New Journalism: A Whole New Proposition." All passages quoted from this unpublished paper are reprinted by permission of the author.

10. What does he dream or fantasize about?

11. How would he react to a common situation—such as when some-one brazenly pushes ahead of him in a cafeteria lineup? What if a subordinate dared to contradict him? (Perhaps you'd like to try that yourself in a devil's advocate role.)

12. What was his childhood like? His parents? What were his child-hood ambitions? To what extent has he fulfilled, exceeded, and/or changed them? What parallels can he draw between childhood and his present life?

13. What is the sand in his oyster: i.e., what annoys the hell out of of him? Conversely, what especially pleases him?

14. Weaknesses or negative traits (you'll get them mostly from inter-viewing others about him or reading previous articles): What does he say about them? What, if anything, is he doing about them?

15. What have been some of the most significant changes in his life? What caused them? How did he cope with them? How does he feel about them now?

As a final point (though it cannot be put in the form of a question) the interviewer must constantly be on the alert for the little things: incidents, "human" characteristics, off-guard remarks—characteristics with which the reader can identify. The great and celebrated man suffers from stage fright when making a speech—how touching! Or the famous black leader, who pontificates about the need for education, stops to ask a small youngster on the street, "How come you're not in school today?"—a touching scene that illustrates his point. Or the tough, cool cop admits that he's terrified as he knocks on the door to answer a call about a family fight—he's human after all. People like to read about human foibles of the great, their weaknesses, their mistakes. It makes the readers feel a little better about themselves.

Pursuing such a set of topics is no guarantee of success. Perhaps the only real formula for success in personality interviewing is a basic appre-ciation for people and a willingness to try hard as an interviewer and as a writer.

It's up to you.

Pete Martin of "I call on . . ." fame used to tell respondents: "If this interview is any good it'll be your doing, not mine. You're the one who has to be intelligent and amusing and funny. I'm just the mouth-piece."

Martin says that line worked fine for awhile. It was Danny Kaye who caught up with him.

"Don't give me that jazz," replied Danny. "If this thing is any good it's going to be you that's doing it. Don't try to hang your burden on me" (*Pete Martin Calls On* . . .).

They're both right, though not totally. In truth, it's a shared responsibility. Creative interviewing, indeed.

TEN

Special Problems

Q. Sergeant, have you ever had to fire your gun? I mean . . .

A. Yes, I certainly have, I—

Q. . . . like, y'know, more than just in target practice, such as maybe you've fired a warning shot, or . . .

A. Yes, there was the time—

Q. . . . . or maybe you've taken a shot at a fleeing bank robber . . .

A. Yes, yes, I've—

Q. . . . or maybe you've had a big gun battle with a fugitive holed up in an abandoned barn out in the country where . . .

A. Yes, that happened once—

Q. . . . Or maybe you're like a lot of other officers who have never fired . . .

Should I use a tape recorder? How do you even *get* an interview with a busy executive? How do I know whether I'm getting a snow job? The following answers are based on experience: my own and that of about a hundred journalists whom I have interviewed. The suggestions presented here, though they may seem didactic, represent the aggregate of all our experiences, probably around one million interviews.

TAKING NOTES

You can't listen, think up questions, and take notes all at once. Therefore you must study very carefully what you need to record via notes. For a verbatim account, use a tape recorder. Shorthand and speedwriting are usually *not* the answer because concentration on the mechanics precludes good conversational rapport.

Should you take notes at all? In 1927, long before tape recorders, foreign correspondent Edward Price Bell said he took no notes during his interviews with major world figures. He wrote his notes afterward, bit by bit as memory served him: "A word or phrase now, a sentence then, perhaps a paragraph or two as one wakes at night. I consider a week or even a fortnight not too long a time to give to the complete reproduction of an interview of some five thousand words."

More recently novelist Truman Capote, researching his nonfiction novel, *In Cold Blood,* said that he trained himself to remember almost verbatim the content of long conversations. He practiced by listening to tapes and then writing down the content afterward.

Murlin Spencer, long-time Associated Press correspondent, is typical of many news writers. He takes notes during interviews but seldom looks at them when writing his story. He merely browses through them afterward to check his memory. "What you retain in your mind should be the most important thing," he explains.

Support for the view comes from one research study (Abel, 1959) that compared notetakers with non-notetakers in ability to recall the content of a seven-minute oral statement. Surprisingly, the non-notetakers were more factually accurate, though less complete, in their recall.

Notetaking is, nonetheless, among the most vital functions of the journalist. Most reporters take their notes on small notebooks such as stenopads. Some use clipboards.

Here are some suggestions:

Record Specific Data

Dates, names, spellings, ages, percentages, and figures must be jotted down. Memories can be relied on for concepts, quotes, and anecdotes, but specific figures are elusive.

Additional Data

Note major points, then specific documentation for those points: facts, figures, anecdotes, instances. If a politician says, "We are losing ground in our fight against violence," the reporter notes that down, then asks "Why? . . . What facts do you have?" He notes those down, too: murder up 24 percent in a year, rape up 18 percent, assault up 12 percent. Some reporters use a system of summarizing major points on one side of a stenopad page and citing the supporting documentation on the other.

This permits a quick grasp of the major elements of a story when writing it.

Develop a Shorthand

Getting a direct quote word for word is the major problem of notetaking. It's complicated by the fact that you don't know whether it's a "memorable" quote until you've heard it. One solution is to train your mind to "hold" a quote in memory until you can write it down. Another is to begin noting down, as it occurs, a comment that starts with such ominous portent that it *seems* likely to be significant ("I want to warn the governor about one thing above all others . . ."). Some form of speedwriting is useful here, such as dropping vowels and using symbols for common words: *ths hlps u gt ur info wrd 4 wrd.*

Slow the Pace

You can slow the interview by asking clarifying probes or "dummy" questions that permit you to catch up with your notes. You can simply slow down the respondent: "Just a moment, Senator—what you say is important. I want to get down every word."

Conversational Discipline

If a respondent says, "I have three reasons for taking this action," the reporter writes down "3 rsns" and makes sure he gets all three before proceeding. The taped interview, by contrast, has a tendency to wander: without notes the interviewer may forget points two and three.

Nonverbal Cues

Notetaking encourages talk in the direction of the most pencil movement. Inexperienced respondents, however, sometimes panic when you start to write. Telling them what you're writing and why it's important can ease you through this problem.

Memory Training

Most journalists, once they get over their insecurities, can train their minds to recall worthy items, thus reducing the need for extensive notetaking. If a quote is truly memorable, you ought to be able to remember it. Sketchy notes may be sufficient. Writing down *567 jacks* in your notes helps you to recall a corny story about the size of jackrabbits in rural Nevada.

Typewritten Notes

The newspaper practice of taking notes by typewriter in face-to-face interviews is among the more extreme examples of inhumanity. It's not so bad on the phone in perfunctory interviews with experienced respondents such as police desk sergeants. A school superintendent, however, says:

> Reporters call you up and the minute you say something you hear that clacking typewriter. It isn't the typing that bothers me so much as what it symbolizes. It means the fine nuances of conversation are lost. Listening becomes mechanical. It's a linear thing rather than total immersion in the conversation. If you so much as utter a burp you activate that darned typewriter!

The increasing newsroom use of video display terminals, electronic typewriters that flash the words onto a TV-like screen above the keyboard, helps to solve the "clacking" problem—they're quiet. But they don't necessarily make listening less mechanical.

Words or Meanings?

Communications theory suggests that words don't mean things, *people* do. An inarticulate respondent may take two hundred words to say what a writer could sum up in twenty. The reporter can alleviate the problem by use of probes to get him to say it a second time more succinctly. It's that second (or third or fourth) statement you write in your notes.

TAPE RECORDERS

Among newspaper writers the tape recorder is an object of intense controversy. The reporter often claims to have no time to transcribe a taped interview. He fears the recorder will intimidate a source and cause him to speak less candidly. And he worries about that Disaster of Disasters, the mechanical breakdown. Let's look at each problem.

Intimidation

It's the skill of the interviewer, not the presence of the machine, that determines whether a source talks candidly. Far from intimidating the source, the recorder permits vastly greater rapport. Freed of the cumbersome mechanics of notetaking, reporters find that they can concentrate for the first time on the fine nuances of conversation. They begin to ask more sensitive and perceptive questions.

"I can really *listen* to the conversation," says one veteran newswriter in Honolulu. This man also learned a harsh lesson about his style of interviewing after listening to his tapes: "I talk too damn much. I'm too impatient. I'm always cutting off my source just as he starts to say something."

Reporters often find, too, that relistening to a tape brings out significant points missed early in the interview; their importance became clear only in the light of subsequent conversation.

Such considerations have brought recorders increasingly into newsrooms across the country. This has been enhanced by development of the pocket recorder, a machine hardly bigger than a fat paperback. It's small enough to slip into a purse or coat pocket. It has become a basic tool of reporting in the 1970s. A pocket recorder is particularly valuable in situations where notetaking is impossible, such as interviewing a jogger on the run. Public figures often prefer reporters to use recorders—there's less risk of being misunderstood or misquoted.

As for intimidation, most respondents take their cues from the interviewer. If you're relaxed and unconcerned about the machine, so are they. The person who must learn to be calm about the recorder, then, is the interviewer himself. The less attention given the machine the better. When interviewing, set it in an inconspicuous position, preferably out of sight. Put the mike close to the respondent but out of the line of sight between you. Turn the machine on early, preferably during the icebreaker stage of conversation. Try not to look at it again; just leave it running.

Some respondents are bothered by one thing: what happens to the tape? If the interview is to cover potentially sensitive or embarrassing points, some reassurance may be necessary at the start of the conversation: the tape is a record of a private conversation between the two of you. No one but you will listen to it, and then only to take notes from it. The tape itself will be erased (i.e., reused) afterward. You must, of course, honor the promise of confidentiality. Some writers who interview celebrities place their tapes in library archives under restrictions that they not be released for a specified time, usually after the death of all parties concerned. Court decisions have suggested that the pledge of confidentiality can be broken by a court subpoena but only when reason exists to believe the tape may shed light on the commission of a serious crime.

Transcribing

The critics are right—it takes an experienced typist three to four hours to transcribe a one-hour tape. Most reporters merely take notes off the tape, using a typewriter. A fast typist who selects carefully can often keep up with the conversation and therefore doesn't have to stop the tape. You may find, too, that you need only a few items from an hour-long tape. If you know where those things are (by noting down, during the conversation, the number on the digital counter that is built into most good tape recorders) you can fast-forward the tape right to those points.

Ten Ways to Avoid Mechanical Disaster

The following suggestions should help you overcome your fears about mechanical mishaps.

1. Once you've bought a sturdy, dependable machine, practice with it by yourself until you become so familiar with it that you can use it without being self-conscious.

2. Keep extra batteries available, particularly for the pocket recorder whose AA cells need replacement about every three hours of record-play time. Rechargeable battery packs are notorious for suddenly running out of power. You'd be wise to invest in extras.

3. Don't run out of tape; carry extra cassettes.

4. Make sure new cassettes roll freely; the cheap ones sometimes stick.

5. Make sure the microphone switch is turned on.

6. Don't record in noisy places: restaurants, cocktail bars, moving cars and planes.

7. Use caution with extra-thin tape (such as in the C–120 cassette); it tangles, slips, breaks, or otherwise malfunctions in some machines.

8. If your machine has no end-of-tape shutoff, keep track of time so you won't run out of tape before you run out of conversation.

9. Guard against accidental re-recording. Label each cassette and remove the "accidental record" tabs.

10. Check your machine before each use like a pilot's preflight check of instruments: (a) batteries okay, (b) cassettes okay, (c) spare batteries and cassettes available, (d) mike switch on, (e) short preinterview trial recording shows record and playback operating okay.

What Kind of Recorder?

Machines suitable for interviewing must be light, portable, and dependable. Two basic types fill this need, the *pocket* and the *portable* cassette machines. Both use regular cassettes, which come in four types depending on playing time: C–30 (fifteen minutes on each side), C–60, C–90, and C–120.

The pocket recorder. It normally weighs less than two pounds and costs from $55 to $175. Most models have an automatic level control (ALC), which automatically adjusts the record level for various intensities of sound. Most have a built-in microphone with provision for external mikes, external input (to record from a radio or another recorder), and a remote switch to stop the machine via footpedal or microphone switch. Most have a light or meter to warn of low batteries. Some have automatic end-of-tape shutoff. Disadvantages of this small machine include a tinny playback sound and a limited power supply that requires frequent change of batteries.

The portable recorder. It's larger, weighing five to seven pounds, and costs $50 to $150. It has the features of the pocket machine and also has what the other lacks: a bigger speaker for playback, longer-lasting power, and built-in adapter for household current. The portable uses from four to six C or D cells, which last anywhere from eight to thirty-five hours, depending on the model and frequency of use.

Two other machines deserve brief mention, though their journalistic use is limited. One is the *mini-recorder,* even smaller than the pocket and more expensive. It's designed for dictating memos on miniature cassettes lasting fifteen minutes to the side. The other is the reel-to-reel machine, almost extinct as a portable. One portable model still available in 1976 uses five-inch reels, costs about $400, and operates at four different tape speeds: from less than one inch per second (ips) to seven ips. Its advantages are higher fidelity at the faster tapes speeds (good for recording music), and longer recording time at the slower speeds (as much as ten hours using both sides of the thin .5-mil tape).

Four accessories should be considered by anyone buying a tape recorder: rechargeable battery packs for those machines that accommodate them, earphones (the big ones, not the single earplug) for private listening to playback, a footpedal to stop the playback when taking notes, and a telephone pickup for recording telephone interviews.

Laws pertaining to the legality of taping telephone conversations are hopelessly confusing. The telephone company says, "In most cases use of a recorder on telephone conversations without the audible beep tone is contrary to the company's tariffs and is not permitted." The exceptions are commercial broadcast stations when the respondent is informed that a recording is being made, and the recording of police and fire emergency calls. Art Spikol describes his extensive investigation to find out exactly what that means ("Taping and Tapping," *Writer's Digest,* April 1976), and says he found no definitive answer either from the company's lawyers or from Public Utility Commission officials in Washington. His conclusion: How is the telephone company going to know you're taping? How can they prove it? Even if they knew, would they be likely to take it to court? He could find no such case that ever went to court. More important are federal and state wiretap laws. Federal law says taping is okay so long as one party knows about it, meaning that it's not necessary to inform the respondent. One study (Riley and Wiessler, 1974) says consent of all parties to a telephone conversation is required before taping can legally be made in seven states: California, Hawaii, Illinois, Maryland, Nevada, Oregon, and Pennsylvania.

GETTING THE INTERVIEW

With busy people, often the most difficult aspect of an interview is getting it. Patience and persistence may pay off, but if not here are some other possibilities:

Work through an intermediary sympathetic to your purpose.

Write a letter specifically outlining your purpose. Tell why you think it would benefit the respondent to be interviewed.

Call him on the phone and start asking questions. This may draw his interest; if not, he may at least answer some of your questions on the phone. A congressman who refused to see me in person ("I don't have one spare minute of time," he explained) spent an hour talking with me via long distance phone.

Seek an opportunity to meet your respondent informally at a public function: a meeting or after a press conference. Celebrities are left "unguarded" surprisingly often at such events. Perhaps a quiet chat will draw his interest in being interviewed.

Find a purpose attractive to him. A show business celebrity who balks at still another routine interview might readily consent to talk about a favorite subject such as volunteer work with troubled teenagers.

Use flattery unabashedly: "Yes, I know you're busy . . . busy people are always the most interesting and important . . . we wouldn't want you otherwise." (Actual words used to convince a balky respondent who replied, with a laugh, "Stop! Stop! I'll *do* it!")

Interview others close to your prospective respondent and let your good work filter back to him.

Arrange to meet informally at some off-hour activity such as an early morning walk.

News reporters have special problems interviewing participants in public crisis or controversy, such as a labor dispute. To persuade reluctant sources, reporters have developed several standard arguments ranging from gentle flattery to threats of bad publicity. Flattery includes such remarks as *the story needs your comments to be complete. . . . A lot of people have asked me about your views and I said I'd try to find out.*

Some news writers use subterfuges, such as pretending to have a great deal of information they don't really have: *I have practically everything I need for this story, but I'd like to get just a comment or two from you.* Another typical ploy is to cite a false but plausible statement that the reporter has picked up from a "reliable source." The respondent hastens to correct the false statement, thereby revealing the facts. A more honest and preferable approach is to ask for "background information to put things in perspective." Given the chance to give that perspective, the source often willingly responds to the sensitive questions he would have avoided in the head-on interviewing approach.

In the "threat" category are such comments as *the story will run anyway, with or without your comments. . . . I'll have to quote you as "refusing comment," which may not look good. . . . If you don't comment now, you'll simply extend a minor embarrassment into a prolonged scandal.*

Such tactics, particularly the subterfuges, should be used discreetly, if at all. They are standard in newsrooms across the country, but reporters might consider using fewer strong-arm tactics and more logical arguments. Many hard-driving reporters force sources into a defensive "no comment" posture simply by being too heavy-handed, impatient, and intolerant.

Often the reporter's best persuasive tactic is a logical argument. An Oregon sportswriter, Blaine Newnham, was covering the Olympics in Munich in 1972. The late runner Steve Prefontaine had finished fourth in the 5,000-meter run, and he wasn't happy about it. He'd never lost a big race before. Newnham had inspected the stadium and knew the athletes had to pass through a certain corridor that he had access to. There he encountered the dejected Prefontaine.

"I've got to talk to you," he told the runner.

"I'm not talking," said Prefontaine. "I don't have anything I want to say."

Newnham had come 6,000 miles from Eugene, Oregon, to watch Prefontaine's performance. He felt he *had* to have this story.

He said, "You talk a lot about this bond you have between yourself and the Eugene track fans. You talk about what all the people in Eugene have done for you. They have thought about this race for four years. They've backed you. They've sat out in the rain watching you. Now they want to know what you think. You can *not* walk away from them now and say you don't want to talk. You owe it to them to talk to them."

Prefontaine was taken aback. Finally he said, "Okay. Let's go over here and sit down."

Newnham, a skilled and sensitive interviewer, started the session with comments designed to rebuild the runner's sagging ego. "You ran a good race. You ran to win. You're fourth best in the world. How bad is that?"

Within five minutes Prefontaine was himself again: "Wait until Montreal—I'll run him [the winner] off the track."

In the final analysis, the best way to get an interview is to have faith in yourself and your purpose. This sense of professionalism and self-confidence will communicate itself to the respondent, even over the phone. It's in your voice. Too many novice interviewers feel that they are so worthless and miserable that no one could possibly want to talk with them. That, too, communicates itself, making it a self-fulfilling prophecy.

COPING WITH HOSTILITY

You defuse hostility by finding the reason for it. The most common reason is *you*—your own scarcely disguised resentment based on prejudging your respondent (you've always hated FBI agents, etc.). You're certainly entitled to be as narrow-minded and bigoted as you wish, but don't expect others to respond with amiable candor. Forget your animosity. Either your source has information you want or he doesn't. If he does, he should be treated with human dignity and respect for his ability to impart that information. If he doesn't have the information you want, stay out of his hair.

If the problem is not you, then one way to defuse hostility is to ask about it: "Just what is it that's bothering you?" That's what one reporter, Ron Bellamy, asked after a fruitless, tense twenty-minute interview with an angry baseball player, Reggie Jackson. In answer the athlete shouted a stream of invectives about the biased reporting of a previous interviewer. The reporter merely listened. Then, remarkably, the interview began anew. Freed of his anger, Jackson talked with new-found candor. "One of the best interviews I ever had," the reporter said afterward.

A good way to eliminate hostility, then, is to puncture it as you'd lance a festering boil. Another way is to set aside points of disagreement. One reporter, interviewing a physician hostile toward the press, said, "Doctor, I won't blame you for the sins of the medical profession if you won't blame me for the sins of the newspaper profession." They got along fine.

Sometimes the hostility is merely an unwillingness to discuss a particular, possibly sensitive topic. Marcosson *(Adventures in Interviewing)* offers this advice: "Start him on some subject remote from the one at hand. This tends to crank up his powers of expression. Before long he unconsciously returns to the thing you really want to talk about and reels off data like a streak."

HOW DO YOU KNOW HE'S TELLING
THE TRUTH?

Truth exists at several levels. Ask a man how he feels and he'll probably say "fine." But in fact his back aches and he has a cough. He feels anxious about his children. He's concerned at middle age about the meaning of his life, the futility and drabness of it. He feels depressed. Was he lying when he said "fine"? Not really. It's just that the "interviewer" didn't probe deeply enough. A superficial, insincere question will get you an equally shallow answer.

If you define truth as a naive kind of factual reality, then several rough measures of it are available to the interviewer.

Sources

Where did he get his information? What factual evidence does he have to support his assertion? Aggressive probing along this line is far from a perfect solution, but it does tend to intimidate liars and persons with "selective memories." Conversely it enhances rapport with those who are leveling with you.

Corroboration

Other persons can verify the statement, or supporting evidence about it exists in written form. The interviewer who has done his homework often *knows* whether he's getting a snow job.

Plausibility

Common sense tells you whether the statement has a ring of reality to it.

Vested Interest

You correct for "windage" if you perceive that the respondent has something specific to gain—such as economic advantage or political leverage—by getting his comments published.

Credibility

You place more trust in comments by persons who have demonstrated over long periods their ability to present unvarnished facts. You also place greater trust in a respondent who gives you correct answers to factual questions for which you already happen to have the answers. You can, indeed, devise "accuracy check" questions as a test of credibility.

Authority

You place more weight on the commentary of those clearly in a position to know: the police chief on crime statistics, for example.

PACING THE INTERVIEW

An interview is not always a totally pleasant, bland encounter. Some of the best may start on a balmy note but quickly move to stormy episodes involving tension, anger, even tears. An interviewer must be alert to the other's feelings and offer changes of pace, easing off on the tension when necessary or, conversely, shifting gears to a more intense level when the interview becomes listless. Such changes of pace give an interview an exciting quality, and the information imparted often reflects this excitement.

NUDGING HAZY MEMORIES

Psychological studies suggest that people remember first things, last things, and unusual things. This helps to explain why such questions as "What was your most frightening experience?" or, "Tell me about some of the unusual things that happened to you" tend to be successful. They are episodes that people can remember in detail. Memory also operates by association. Psychologists say everything that happens to us is stored in memory, but cues from the environment are required to find an entrance into that storage area.

So the interviewer seeking to discuss events of the past comes armed with cues. Some may be topics of the era: "We're talking about 1964, the year of the first major student uprising at Berkeley." Personal cues also help: "That was the year you vacationed at the dude ranch in Colorado."

If it's specific detail you want, ask a woman. Novelist Arthur Hailey told TV interviewer Jeanne Wolf in 1975 that he finds women better than men at recalling anecdotal and personal detail—the kind of thing most writers are seeking. The observation is supported by a research study at Ohio Wesleyan University (Bahrick, 1975) that showed women respondents generally superior to men in ability to recall years later the names and faces of high school classmates.

Memories must be treated with delicacy. To ask a witness six months after a tragedy, "Where was the train when the bus stalled on the tracks?" may invite inaccurate recall. Better to ask, "Tell me what you remember of the train wreck," and let the witness reconstruct it as best he can. When he's finished you can go over his story with gentle probing for associated memories; one thing leads to another like falling dominoes.

Careful advance preparation is essential. You must come to the interview with letters, clippings, memoranda, and reports in hand. If you make copies available to the respondent beforehand, both of you will come prepared.

EVASIVENESS

You cope with evasiveness precisely the same way you cope with poison ivy. You learn first to recognize it. It appears in many forms. Among them are answering questions other than the ones asked, giving opinions or hopelessly vague abstractions instead of facts, and answering questions with questions. You'll also find selective memories, filibustering, browbeating, and derailment ("But the *basic* issue is really this . . ." says the respondent who proceeds to throw your whole line of questioning off the track). Once you recognize an evasion, you eradicate it with a vengeance. Keep track of your question. If you don't get an answer, ask again. And again.

A word of caution: The tough approach is more oriented to public officials than to private citizens. A reporter should feel he has a right to try to pin down a slippery mayor on a matter of public interest. He should not badger a private citizen—a witness to a tragedy, for example—whose evasiveness stems from trauma or inarticulateness.

THE NEWS CONFERENCE

The news conference is a necessary means of transmitting news, particularly in large cities where officials simply cannot afford the time to grant individual interviews to a dozen different reporters. It is not an effective arena for the skilled interviewer. No opportunity exists to establish rapport. Hostility and tension often operate against candor. Follow-up questions are hard to ask. A skilled and well-prepared interviewer would be foolish to ask a perceptive question only to hear or read the answer first in a competing medium. Mike Thoele, a prize-winning newspaper feature writer in Oregon, says he's asked only one major question at press conferences in ten years of professional work. That was when another reporter asked the district attorney a question that seemed to lead toward premature release of information that Thoele had worked hard to obtain exclusively. Rather than let the entire news corps stumble unwittingly into his private goldmine, Thoele quickly asked a "diversionary" question to throw the conversation off in another direction. It worked.

OFF THE RECORD

A reporter asks an official, "What do you think of the governor's latest proposal for school support?"

"I'm certainly going to study it with keen interest in the weeks ahead," he replies. Then, he confides, "But off the record, I think the governor is a silly fool for making so outrageous a suggestion."

Assuming he's agreed to go off the record, the reporter will quote the first statement, not the second. But he's also obtained a valuable news tip. He'll call several other officials, and if they all strongly oppose the governor's proposal, he has another worthwhile story. Sooner or later he'll find people willing to say so for publication. So some use exists for the "off the record" policy, even from the journalist's viewpoint.

When some respondents, particularly the inexperienced, say "off the record," they often mean varying things. The strict definition of the term is that statements made off the record are simply not to be published. They are intended only for the reporter's background information. Officials go off the record for various reasons—they are reluctant to indulge in personality squabbles or they want to avoid premature disclosure of forthcoming events. A police chief, answering questions about enforcement of drug laws, places off the record the announcement of a forthcoming crackdown on drug pushers. Publication would obviously drive pushers deeper underground.

But sometimes they mean "not for attribution": that statements may be published but without attribution to the source. News columns are full of "sources said" or "according to reliable sources." Sometimes this is an official sending up a trial balloon (the "source" is the official himself). Or it may be someone who fears that identification may damage him in some way. A cop who discusses low morale in the police department may be reprimanded if his name is used with his published observations.

And sometimes respondents mean that the interview is totally confidential but that the information may be used as "general intelligence" in special ways. Novelist Arthur Hailey interviewed prominent bankers and auto manufacturers with the understanding that the material would be woven into a work of fiction in a way that no source is identifiable. Studs Terkel has said that many of the interviews he did for *Hard Times* and *Working* were of a confidential nature, though some respondents have said later that they'd have preferred to have their names known. A new trend toward candor exists today. In the book *The First Time* such celebrities as Loretta Lynn, Debbie Reynolds, and Dr. Benjamin Spock reveal candidly the most intimate details of their often-awkward first sexual experiences. The book is a monument to the new candor being achieved through interviews.

In light of this candor, many news writers find the off-the-record syndrome a nuisance. Some frankly tell sources that if they don't want certain statements published they shouldn't say them. They've found, surprisingly, that many statements go back on the record. The sources are anxious to tell anyway. Reporters are also wary of getting trapped into promising to go off the record only to hear things they already have (or could easily obtain) from other sources.

Many newspaper editors also abhor what they see as a growing trend toward the anonymous source. They have encouraged writers either to identify the source or to eliminate the anonymous statement. An unidentified source is always a little suspect, and some editors feel that news media credibility is none too high anyway. Sometimes, however, it's the only way to get information. *Washington Post* reporters Carl Bernstein and Bob Woodward enforced a rule during their investigation of the Watergate affair that each confidential statement be corroborated by at least one additional source before it could be published. A good policy.

WHAT ARE YOU PLANNING TO WRITE ABOUT ME?

How candid should you be in discussing the purpose of your interview? I've consistently advocated interviewer candor in return for respondent candor. Not everyone will agree. Some see the interview as a grand poker game whose major attribute is the bluff or the con job. I can only suggest that what such journalists frequently get in return is a con job, a snow job, or a reluctance to talk. That's especially true the second time around, after the respondent has learned a painful lesson. When truth falters, as it often does in poker, the reader is cheated.

True, the writer will find many wily politicians and bureaucrats who play their own brand of journalistic poker. Even they often grudgingly respect honesty—or they're scared to death of it. Some wily bureaucrats learned their tricks from reporters. I know one who started his job with naive honesty. A public crisis came up, unfortunately, and the reward for this sincere candor was to be "burned" again and again as reporters sensationalized his remarks or took them out of context. He quickly lost his naivete—and his candor—and another "wily bureaucrat" was born.

When a respondent asks, "What do you plan to write about me?" the correct answer is, "I don't know." It's the only honest answer you can give. If you knew what you planned to write, you'd be at the typewriter. In an interview you should be seeking answers. When the evidence is in, *then* you'll know what to write. So probably will the respondent if he's the major source and if you're a good interviewer. He'll sense it in the kinds of follow-up questions you ask.

Should you let the source see what you've written before publication? News writers for daily papers usually say, "No." It's too much fuss, they say, when working against a tight deadline. The source is often super-sensitive and emotionally distraught, particularly if the issue is volatile and controversial. But when the writer has more time, such as in magazine articles or newspaper features, some writers have no objection so long as the source understands that the review is *for accuracy only*.

THE MEDIA FREAK

You won't be in business long as an interviewer before encountering the media freak, a person whose every utterance is coldly calculated to get attention in the news media. He has seriously studied the media, and he claims to know their every weakness. He uses a weakness to his advantage. He knows, for example, that the media love confrontation. He knows that they prefer attackers to defenders, fighters to lovers, high profile to low, violence to peace, simple solutions to complex, hard action to soft philosophy.

The media freak doesn't merely talk, he hurls challenges and verbal exclamation points. He uses plain Anglo-Saxon words. He attacks institutions, such as big government, the party in power, corporations, big publishers. He talks slowly for pad and pencil reporters or in thirty-second staccato bursts for TV. He has well-oiled duplicating equipment for news releases and press kits. He "hates" editors and "loves" reporters because he knows that it's the reporters who get stories into the papers, not the editors. Besides, it's fashionable today to hate editors. He is always good for a colorful quote. I asked one self-admitted media freak, a politician, if his activities didn't add up to "manipulation."

> *Manipulation?* If I manipulate the press, that's like two lovers playing with each other for their mutual enjoyment. Editors don't like me very much. One editor likes to think of me as a character; he doesn't like to think of me as having substance. He said once, "Look at all the space we've given you," and I said, "Space, hell! I've given you *news*. Good, solid news." Well, that's an editor for you. With reporters, we have a hell of a fine time.

THE BORING RESPONDENT

What happens if the respondent is a hopeless bore? I gave up trying to answer that question after lecturing on interviewing to a group of house organ editors. An attractive young woman came up later to ask what advice I had for coping with bores. I started to answer, but to my astonishment I could see that I was *boring* her! Boredom, I'm now convinced, is in the eye of the beholder. The late A. J. Liebling once remarked, "Reporting by and large is being interested in everyone you meet." The woman said she was tired of writing articles about retiring employees. She'd ask, "What are your hobbies?" The guy says he likes to fish. "How boring," she thinks. "What a cliché." The creative interviewer, by contrast, would press further. How many fish had he caught in fifty years? What interesting fishing experiences has he had? Has he any "fish tales" or legends or lore he can relate? What's happened to sports fishing in the last half-century? The answers might be fascinating. You might unlock astonishing insights—you might not, of course, but you have to try. *Everybody* has at least one interesting insight or experience to pass along to the rest of the world. It's the interviewer's job to rise to the challenge and find it.

ELEVEN

Interviewing Exercises

Q. I'd like to start by asking some questions
about yourself, some of them personal,
some of them not, as for example it's
necessary or at least desirable for the
reader to possess certain kinds of information, that is, you know, if the reader knows
something about the era you represented
as a child and the kind of environment
encountered during your childhood, he or
she would understand some things about
that person's outlook on life, and . . . .

A. Are you asking when and where I grew
up?

Q. Well, you know, it's important for the—

A. I was born in Sandusky, Ohio, June 10,
1932. I was a depression baby, and my
most vivid recollection as a kid was World
War II. For heaven's sake, why don't you
just ask your questions, and let's get on
with it?

You can't learn it all from a book. One way to learn is to start asking
questions—or better yet, answering them. Nothing is more revealing to
the novice interviewer than to *be* interviewed, especially by someone
equally inexperienced.

Chances are you'll learn more from a bad interview than a good. A
skilled interviewer is so smooth that the process looks deceptively easy.

How different are the wayward efforts of the novice interviewer. Class-room exercises in our interviewing seminar—a simple pairing of students with instructions to one to obtain certain kinds of specific information from the other—illustrate the point. By being interviewed, students learn the importance of clearly stating the purpose at the beginning. "I thought you wanted to know my political views in *general*," said one student-respondent after an interview. "If you wanted to know how I plan to vote in the next election, why didn't you just *say* so?"

A typical reaction.

When the classroom interview respondents were asked to "tell a funny story," they realized how nearly impossible that is. When they heard vague or convoluted questions, they learned to sharpen their own questions. One young woman spent fifteen frustrating minutes trying to answer questions about her views on wilderness conservation. The interviewer thought she'd done a lot of wilderness backpacking. Eventually she confessed that she'd been hiking only once in her life, a seven-hour trail hike that gave her sore legs, footblisters, and a disenchantment about outdoors adven-ture. A simple filter question at the start—how much hiking have you done?—would have cleared that up in a hurry.

A CASE HISTORY

Let's look at an example. One of our graduate students, Margaret Laine, had worked as an epidemiologist for the health department in Oklahoma City. Her job was to investigate cases of venereal disease in order to prevent its spread. The job required extensive interviewing under diffi-cult circumstances—not all people want to reveal their sexual activities—to determine the identity of sexual "contacts." The job also required going out into the "field"—often to the worst parts of town—to find some vaguely identified person whom she then encouraged to go to a clinic for examination and possible treatment.

Margaret seemed the ideal interview respondent, a personable and articulate young woman whose work sounded interesting, even exciting and hazardous. She'd been interviewed before by Oklahoma newspaper reporters writing feature stories about her work.

We sent her out of the classroom so that out of her hearing we could set a purpose and structure for the interview. We decided to ask her to describe the interview techniques she used in her investigative work. We knew that she'd undergone intensive interview training for her work and that she had used interviews in seeking to identify "contacts" who might be spreading the infection. We imagined that she could enlighten us about interviewing under less-than-ideal conditions, perhaps even tell us interesting interviewing experiences. All we had to do was ask.

A young man volunteered to start the interview. When Margaret reentered the room she did not, of course, know the purpose we'd established. She sat in a chair across a conference table from the interviewer; another dozen students sat around the table as observers. Here is the verbatim transcript of the interview. (The Q-numbers are reference points for the interview analysis that follows the transcript.)

Q-1. I'd like to ask you some questions about your job as a VD investigator in Oklahoma City.

A. Okay.

Q-2. Okay, I think I'd like to start out not by trying necessarily to pin you down in your own experiences but in some of your impressions of the most successful techniques you used for getting the information you wanted. . . .

A. You mean—

Q-3. Ah, your contacts that, ah, or other contacts that you found that were the, ah . . . (silence) . . . when you go out and meet someone, you ran into someone we'll say was kind of hard to talk to. . . .

A. Uh-huh—

Q-4. . . . what did you find worked most successfully in getting through to them. . . .

A. Okay, I—

Q-5. . . . in terms of loosening them up to the point where they'd, you know, be willing to go along with whatever it is you wanted them to do?

A. Are you talking about the regular interviews with someone who has venereal disease or are you talking about. . . .

Q-6. Right.

A. . . . trying to find someone in the field?

Q-7. Well, we understood that you went out and contacted people . . . or did you have a number coming in. . . .

A. Uh—

Q-8. . . . volunteers. . . .

A. Okay. Well, it's a combination of both, and two highly different situations. Some people came into the clinic with VD, and anybody who came into the clinic, we talked to them while they were at the clinic. That was the formal interviewing situation. Going out in the field was to find people who had been exposed to VD and to get them into the clinic. It was not an interviewing situation, more a finding situation.

Q-9. How did you get word on them?

A. From the people that came into the clinic or from private hospitals or private doctors or from laboratories.

Q-10. When you went out would you pick a particular time of day you thought would be most successful, I mean, you probably wouldn't go out at night—

A. Yeah, you'd go at night sometimes. Of course, lots of people would be home at night that weren't home during the day. . . .

Q-11. Uh-huh.

A. Ah . . . (silence). . . .

Q-12. So the time of day wouldn't have much to do with it—when you're going out?

A. Well, it had a *lot* to do with it when you're going out. It varied in each case.

Q-13. Did you work all hours?

A. Yeah, you pretty much had your own hours. Your job was to do the job, and sometimes it was done before five, and sometimes you just went swimming and you did it at night. It just depends on who you were looking for and when. We worked every morning.

Q-14. Can you give me some idea of what would happen during an initial contact, say, someone who's not particularly glad to see you?

A. (Chuckles) . . . That's kind of a hard question to answer because, ah, many, many different things would happen. If you kind of narrow it down to—

Q-15. Sort of, type of person?

A. Yeah, type of person, or someone who's angry or someone who's crying or someone who is belligerent, you know; I don't know exactly what you're looking for.

Q-16. Let's say someone who is belligerent. . . . older than you, who is belligerent. Male.

A. Okay, that I've gone out to look for?

Q-17. Uh-huh.

A. And . . . okay, let me think if I can remember an instance like that. . . . there were lots of them, of course, ah. . . . the way you handle it, of course, just depends on the situation. . . . okay. . . . in this one particular instance, I went out in the country. . . . (She tells, with great animation and gesturing, how she'd visited a woman on the front porch of a dilapidated shack in rural Oklahoma. She was chased away by the woman's husband who said threateningly, "Best be gittin' off my land before I get my gun." As Margaret beat a hasty retreat, she heard three shots, one of which shattered the window of her car. "I don't know if he was shooting to hit me or just to scare me, but I wasn't gonna hang around to find out." An entertaining story.)

Q-18. Have any of you ever been shot?

A. And killed, you mean?

Q–19. Well, I'd just settle for wounded.

A. Not in Oklahoma. One guy got beat up but nobody actually got wounded.

Q–20. . . . (silence). . . .

Up to this point, not one word has come out about the uses of interviewing in her job. A careful rereading of the transcript will reveal that the two are actually on different wavelengths. Margaret confirmed this after the interview was over; she hadn't really understood the purpose of the interview. The conversation suffers from other problems: lack of direction, convoluted questions, inadequate listening, lack of real rapport. Below is a question-by-question analysis.

Q–1: The interview is off to a bad start because the purpose is not made clear at the beginning. Margaret said afterward that she had perceived the purpose to be "my experiences as a VD investigator in Oklahoma City." That's what he had said at the beginning; it's what she remembered at the end. At no time, she said later, did she become aware of the real purpose: to inquire about *interviewing* experiences. Careful examination of the rest of the transcript reveals that the two parties continued to misread one another. The problem could easily have been avoided had he explained, "I want to ask how you used the interview in your job, and I'm particularly interested in ideas and experiences that might be useful to members of this class." He could have followed with preliminary filter questions: "How often did you use the interview in your work? . . . In what ways did you use it? . . . How important was it for getting the information you needed? . . . Did you receive any training in interviewing before you started? . . ."

Q–2: This would have been another good time to explain the purpose more specifically.

Q–3: The interviewer, responding to her puzzled expression, hastens to explain but with limited success.

Q–4 through Q–8: Confusion reigns as the parties try to understand one another. The interviewer was misinformed (not his fault) about the role interviews played in her work and the circumstances in which they took place. Margaret said after the interview: "I could see that he didn't understand what I did, so I had to explain the two different aspects of my work."

Q–9: Her explanation should have cleared up the confusion. Unfortunately, the interviewer chose to pursue a tangent. Had he made it clear that he was interested in interviewing experiences, he could have followed up with general questions that lead to specifics: "What kind of information did you usually seek through interviews? . . . What kinds of persons did you talk with? . . . Young? Old? Men? Women? Well educated? . . . Were some harder to interview than others? . . . What kinds were hardest? . . . Did you have specific ways to approach them? . . . What ways? . . . What if those ways didn't work? . . ."

Q–10: Another diversion further diffuses the already unclear direction of questioning.

Q–12: Perhaps a little panicky at the momentary silence, the interviewer throws in a "recap" question—which unfortunately suggests that he hadn't listened very well.

Q–13: Further diversionary entanglement.

Q–14: He tries to get back to the task at hand, but he's hampered by her misperception of purpose. She thought all along that he wanted "experiences," which she interpreted to mean anecdotes. At this point (she explained afterward) she found her mind racing through a lot of experiences trying to locate an incident that seemed to fit. She was still not aware that *interviewing* experiences were being sought. He does not appear to perceive that she is operating on a different wavelength.

Q–15 and 16: Even here, hope remained. He could have replied, "I'm looking for *interviewing* experiences. How, for example, would you approach a belligerent person?"

Q–17: He allows the conversation to stray further, though he gains an entertaining if irrelevant story. He should have replied, "No, I'm talking about the formal interviewing situation at the clinic."

Q–18: Having seemingly abandoned his original purpose, he now merely dives for what glitters. It is possible that Margaret could have revealed experiences and ideas *related to interviewing* that are equally glittering and exciting—and more useful to an interviewing class. We'll never know. She was never asked.

INTERVIEWING EXERCISES

Out of such wayward trials and errors students learn significant lessons. The key to learning is the reaction of the respondents in postinterview critique sessions; their comments often reveal the major problems dramatically. The practice interview exercises below are designed for classrooms where students pair off and interview each other. They normally require about fifteen to twenty minutes of interviewing time. They are among the most successful ones developed in five years of trial and error in our interviewing seminars at the University of Oregon—"successful" in that they are likely to turn up common interviewing faults in ways that can easily be perceived by respondents or classroom observers. Five preliminary principles are important.

1. Interviews must be "real"—no role playing. Everyone must be himself so that scrupulous honesty in personal relationships is maintained.

2. Preparation for each interview must be done out of earshot of the respondents to avoid adulterating the interview.

3. Classroom atmosphere for postinterview discussion must be psychologically safe for even the most timid students; caustic criticism and sarcasm should be discouraged.

4. Each student should fill out a personal background questionnaire to be made available to interviewers for preinterview preparation. Among the points to be covered:

   a. Name, address, age, hometown.

   b. Favorite sports, hobbies, foods, beverages.

   c. Most interesting places visited.

   d. Favorite "fantasies" (students are usually candid and revealing).

   e. A favorite childhood activity.

   f. A frightening or embarrassing moment in one's life.

   g. Plans for future.

   h. Two topics about which the person has specialized knowledge and would enjoy being interviewed.

   i. Details of how specialized knowledge was gained.

5. A postinterview questionnaire should be prepared to permit each respondent to evaluate each of the following points on a rating scale, with space provided for suggestions.

   a. Purpose of interview made clear?

   b. Questions clearly stated?

   c. Questions always relevant to stated purpose?

   d. Interviewer a good listener?

   e. Rapport okay (you felt comfortable and relaxed)?

   f. You felt free to be honest and candid?

Exercise 1

Ask respondent to enumerate the specific *things* with which he surrounds himself: clothes, books, trinkets, jewelry, mementoes, tape recorders, stereos, cars, photo albums, clippings, old love letters—the list is endless. *Purpose:* Encourage interviewers to seek concrete details that help define and characterize a person. *Suggestions:* The interview can be dull if it merely catalogs things. It can be improved by asking *about* some of the things: they obviously have meaning to the respondent and thereby provide clues to character. Don't forget numbers: the person who keeps four love letters is dramatically different from the one who keeps four hundred. Interviewer should take notes or perhaps use a tape recorder (see "file" below).

Exercise 2

Same as above except interviewer asks for "heroes": the kinds of people the respondent most admires. Could be statesmen, living or dead, authors, celebrities, even less-known persons: parents, friends, teachers.

Exercise 3

Solicit the expressions of an opinion on a topic about which respondent has strong feelings to obtain lively, character-revealing quotes. *Purpose:* Encourages interviewer to seek ways to bring out personality through quotes. *Suggestions:* Prepare by using background questionnaire for clues. Interviewer may ask provocative questions to stimulate colorful quotes. Also try using silence: You ask a question, get an answer—then, silence. See if it works.

Exercise 4

Same as Exercise 3, except interviewer also attempts to find a specific instance or anecdote as further documentation of the "strong feeling." *Purpose:* Encourages interviewer to develop skills in eliciting anecdotes, one of the hardest tasks for the novice. *Suggestions:* See Chapter 4 on anecdotes.

Exercise 5

Explore a topic that holds some sensitivity to respondent, such as a frightening or embarrassing experience or a colorful and private "fantasy." *Purpose:* Interivewer learns to cope with people's feelings. *Suggestions:* You have to play it by ear when dealing with potentially sensitive points. Indirection may help in testing the wind. However, most student-respondents freely discuss such things (or they wouldn't have listed them on the questionnaire). Warm rapport helps.

Exercise 6

Explore with respondent the "specialized knowledge" that he listed in the personal background questionnaire. *Purpose:* Interviewer is usually thrust into an area about which he knows little, which forces him to ask filter and background questions to gain understanding. *Suggestions:* It looks more intimidating than it really is. Most respondents enjoy playing the role of "teacher" on a favorite topic, especially if they have a good "student."

The Interview File

Each interview should produce a "file": semiorganized notes, similar to those provided by magazine correspondents, that may be combined with other files for a roundup story. The file is not a finished story, just notes on specific details, facts, figures, quotes, instances, anecdotes. For an example of a student-produced file, see Appendix.

Out-of-Class Interviews

Interviews done outside the classroom should have a practical purpose if possible. The possibility of publication is a tremendous incentive to both the interviewer and the respondent—though it also puts pressure on both (questions of accuracy, completeness, confidentiality, etc.). Often arrangements can be made for possible publication. Our interviewing groups often took assignments to do "leg" work in connection with planned articles, such as interviews with professors about the changes they'd perceived in students over a ten-year period. Another group conducted taped "oral history" interviews with persons familiar with early days of university history. Another interviewed female professors and staff workers at the university for a "status of women" group preparing a book on the subject. Below are some other standard ideas for out-of-class interviews.

Exercise 7

Interview a senior citizen about the Great Depression era of the 1930s (or some other past era, such as World War II). *Purpose:* To develop techniques of memory stimulation as well as general interviewing experience. This could be part of a feature article. *Suggestions:* Once stimulated, most people love to talk about the past. Read Studs Terkel's *Hard Times* for background on the Depression.

Exercise 8

Interview a working journalist on the ways in which he or she utilizes the interview. (Alternative: Interview other persons who regularly use interviews: a social worker, doctor, nurse, counselor, employment recruiter, police detective.) *Purpose:* Students gain ideas about interviewing by learning how the professionals do it. The best reports can be duplicated for distribution to the class, thus giving the assignment some usefulness. (See Janis Johnson file, Appendix.)

Exercise 9

Interview someone—perhaps a senior citizen—about a tradition of the old days (such as a Fourth of July parade) or how something was done in days gone by (such as running a steam locomotive or a paddlewheel steamer). *Purpose:* Sharpen skills in obtaining details of past events. *Suggestions:* Read *The Foxfire Book,* anthologies of interviews done by high school students with older relatives in rural Georgia. (Alternate assignment: interview workers about their jobs as in Studs Terkel's *Working.*)

Exercise 10

A see-in-action interview. Find a respondent who's willing to have the interviewer observe as he does a task involving much action. Examples: a coach during a game, a judge during a courthouse session, an airport control tower operator on a busy Sunday, a police radio dispatch officer, an exotic dancer, a police officer on patrol (some departments allow observers to ride with officers). *Purpose:* To sharpen interviewer's powers of observation and writing techniques for description and narration. Possible newspaper feature story. *Suggestions:* You have to work in your questions as best you can because often you cannot interrupt the action. Also ask them before and after the action. See Chapter 9 on "saturation reporting" (page 107).

Miscellaneous Exercises

Of course you'll think of other exercises—asking about interesting places visited, about plans for the future, about opinions on events or issues in the news. If it's newswriting class, many other possibilities come to mind for in-class exercises, though most of them involve role playing because students do not normally possess "hard news" information. One exercise is to divide the class into interviewer-respondent pairs and give each respondent a mock police report on an incident such as a routine traffic fatality. Each interviewer must get the necessary information for a news story not by inspecting the report but by asking questions. This is hard, particularly if the respondent does not volunteer information. Another exercise is to ask four or five members of the class to form a "legislative council" that is empowered to make a decision (such as whether the instructor should give a midterm quiz in place of a difficult writing assignment).

The council completes its deliberations in private and then the remaining students are instructed to interview one or more participants individually to "get the story," including details of what was said and how the council arrived at its decision. The council deliberations should be tape recorded and the tape played after the interviews are complete and stories written. The disparity between the witness accounts gained through the interviews and the actual discussion as revealed by the tape is frequently astounding. Reporters often find that what they obtained through the interviews was a mere fragment of the total story. They also learn that witnesses are not always reliable in their recall of specific details.

Appendix

Note: The interview report or "file" is essentially rough or semiorganized notes from the conversation. It includes background details of the respondent, along with comments, quotes, anecdotal material, etc., in line with the purpose of the interview.

Interview Report [1]

Subject: Ann Baker, reporter at the *Eugene Register-Guard*
Interviewer: Janis Johnson
Topic of Interview: Uses of the interview
Background: Ann Baker is a 1970 graduate of the University of Oregon School of Journalism. She began reporting in 1970 at the *Ashland Daily Tidings* as a general assignment reporter. In February of 1971, after seven months at the *Daily Tidings,* she joined the staff of the *Eugene Register-Guard.* In five years at the *Guard,* she has worked her way up from writing the church page and obituary column to being in charge of covering Springfield, an adjacent community. Ann covers Springfield government and sometimes writes general feature stories.

Ann comments on the importance of the interview to her work: "That's all there is to journalism—well, three-fourths, anyway. You do get some information from personal observation, at meetings, or speeches, for example. But 75 percent is talking to someone to get information, facts, or opinions."

As a beat reporter, Ann does a lot of short interviews, some depth interviews, as well as many by telephone. The short interviews are to discuss meeting agendas, to get further information or clarification about

---

[1] Janis Johnson, "Interview Report: Ann Baker," an unpublished paper. Reprinted by permission of the author.

something that happened, or to get a reaction to a charge. For this activity, which was to comprise three-fourths of her work, Ann found herself ill-prepared by her college education:

"I had no real training for interviewing. I suppose I learned it in the process of taking a reporting class. I don't really remember a specific lecture on the subject. The training wasn't enough, whatever it was."

Unfortunately, the *Register Guard* does not provide any on-the-job training sessions for cub reporters. Ann says one of her biggest problems is a personal one—shyness.

"As a reporter, you really have to be aggressive. If you're shy it's really hard. Getting in touch with people, running up to officials after a meeting to get information is important . . . but, it's hard."

An interview, once arranged, has to be prepared for. Aside from backgrounding herself on the topic, Ann still types out a prepared list of questions.

"I have prepared questions, but I don't follow them in order during an interview. In fact, I just remember what the questions are. As long as the interview is going along and the person is talking, it's fine. Then when I have no more questions to ask, I'll consult my list. Most of the time new questions pop up during the interview."

But even with prepared questions, it can be difficult for the new reporter to do a thorough job of interviewing. Ann explains:

"It's that problem of being aggressive. I can ask the tough question. I can get it out, but if they don't give a satisfactory answer I have a tendency to just drop it. I don't continue to ask it until they've answered it to my satisfaction. Sometimes I don't recognize the problem at the time. Usually, I think I'm being very thorough and asking all the right questions, but when I go to write the story, I see huge, gaping holes in it."

What about taking notes versus using a recorder?

"I still have problems getting complete notes that I can read. My notes are just scribbles. For short phone interviews, I just take notes on the typewriter. When I'm going out to do an interview, for a feature, I've been taking the recorder more and more, if I have time to transcribe it. But if I'm doing the interview this afternoon and I have to have the story tomorrow morning, I'll sometimes tape it, but usually won't transcribe it. I'll use it as back up for my notes."

Normally, Ann takes notes even when she is using a recorder.

"I haven't gotten to the point where I can trust the tape recorder completely. In almost every case I take notes too. Once I had my recorder fail. Another time I was interviewing the mayor of Springfield—Vance Freeman—and I was using the recorder and no notes. Just as he was telling a great anecdote, the tape ran out. I couldn't get him to repeat it the same way again, of course, and I'd *never* trust my memory for a direct quote."

How does the recorder seem to affect people's willingness to talk and give direct quotes?

"Sometimes the recorder can inhibit people, but usually they get used to it eventually. Sometimes just the presence of a tape recorder makes people not challenge how you quote them. People's reactions to a recorder can be amusing. I was interviewing someone the other day—a teacher out at Springfield who was forming a new citizen's group to challenge the city council. Every time he'd say something he didn't want me to quote, he'd stick his thumb over the mike. It didn't do any good. It still came through.

"About quotes—that's hard for me and for a lot of reporters. It's difficult to write down direct quotes. You're writing down a quote. You get halfway through it and then they're saying something else that's good, so you go on to the next quote, and you end up missing part of a quote!"

What's the solution?

"I get a full quote when I can, but usually I just get partial quotes." Ann describes herself as a purist on accurate quotes. "I think any time you have direct quotes in quotation marks, you'd better have the person's exact words. I'm more of a purist than some people. There are a lot of differing opinions at the *Guard* about how pure you should be on quotes."

Even a purist may have problems: "I've had people accuse me of misquoting them or taking quotes out of context. One city councilman a couple of months ago just floored me. He said he wanted to give me a compliment. He was referring to a story I'd done earlier in the week. He said, 'You know, that was the very first time you ever quoted me accurately. Congratulations!' "

Ann feels that getting examples and anecdotes from people is as important as getting quotes.

"Examples are important to a story. The personality profile I'm writing of the mayor of Springfield is a good case in point. I turned it in and I had a *few* examples and anecdotes. But I got it back with, 'Let's have some anecdotes.' They're hard to get. What do you do? Call up his friends and say, 'Do you have some good anecdotes about the mayor?' They probably do have some, but thinking of them is hard. I can't do it like that. Another approach that doesn't work is, 'Give some examples.' Usually it works better if you ask people specific questions—really basic ones: 'Where were you born? What kind of a town was that? What kind of family life did you have?' People respond better to specific questions than general ones. That's something I forget a lot. Usually in the course of discussing something, they will try to support what they say with examples."

What about asking the sensitive questions?

"I try to slip those in very late in the interview. You save the tough questions till last. Use the easy questions to get them talking and relaxed and trusting. Then you sock it to them at the end."

What if the person refuses to answer the sensitive question?

"That depends. It depends on how badly you need the information. If you're dealing with a public official, I would usually say, 'Don't you think you have an obligation to tell the public that?' If it's a business-man talking about his business, he really has no obligation to. Then I say, 'You know such and such is really interesting; I think a lot of people could relate to that. Could I get a quote on that?' They usually say it's okay. Sometimes I have to say there was no comment. They usually come out looking worse—as if they have something to hide. But asking if they have something to hide does not work!"

Ann remembers one case where a "no comment" turned into a full-fledged interview:

"I did a series of stories on teenage drinking habits. I called one junior high vice-principal and was trying to get some information about the problem—whether there *was* a problem in that junior high or not. She was very suspicious, very reluctant to talk. She said, 'If we have a problem, we'll take care of it ourselves. We're not going to discuss this in the newspaper.' She went on and on. And when she was through, she said, 'I don't want you to use my name or the name of my school in your story.' I told her it was a little late for that. I told her that when you are speaking off the record, you have to say that *before* you talk. She said she'd never dealt with the press before and didn't understand that. She didn't think it was fair. I didn't handle her very well. I should have stuck to my guns and said, 'That's tough!' But I said I'd think about it and decide later. Luckily, I didn't have to make the decision. She changed her mind and let me come out and talk to her."

Do elected officials ever get difficult to deal with? "Definitely. Once one council member charged another with trying to organize a secret meeting. I had to call him up and get his response to the charge. He was *just* furious. He said, 'Do you have to record it every time we drink a cup of coffee together?' He started accusing me of making up facts. I got very upset. I found it really hard to continue the interview. I was so flustered, I was on the verge of tears, so I didn't get a good response from him. I did get the main idea down, which was essentially, 'No comment.'"

Then are elected officials the hardest people to interview?

"No, the bureaucrats are the hardest. (She defined bureaucrats as hired employees who work in government, usually staff members.) Most of them are working for elected officials and they see their role as feeding *them* information and advice. They think the elected officials should make the public statements. The city manager I'm dealing with is like that. He's cooperative, but to try to get him to make any kind of a strong statement is like pulling teeth. Then there are people who are not public officials at all. Maybe they're in public life, but they're just starting out, or they haven't had much experience, and they feel very uncomfortable in an interview. I've had some very uncomfortable interviews with people who are just scared to death of what you're going to print about them. I try to put them at ease, let them know I'm not going to make them look foolish. When they get uptight like that they just don't say anything good."

Ironically, Ann feels the people she relates to best are among the hardest to interview. "Some of the most intelligent, educated people have a tendency to weigh everything they say. They're careful. They don't want to sound bad. They're the ones who might want you to read the interview back to them. As a policy, we don't let them see it. They'd precensor it, and you'd have no story. But really, that concept is changing now. I think sometimes it's just a good idea to drop the story off with the person, not to see if they agree with it, but to see if you got everything right. Of course, I'd only change a fact error."

Who, then, are the easiest to interview? "The unsophisticated, the nutty people. They are willing to talk; they are enthusiastic and not embarrassed to say things."

Does interviewing get easier as a reporter gains experience? "One thing now is easier for me: I don't get taken in by people as much now. I'm more skeptical and more apt to probe and question. But really easier? No. I think it gets tougher as you go along. You know more what you're supposed to do and what you're doing wrong. That makes it *seem* harder, to say the least."

References, Sources, and Selected Bibliography

ABEL, FRIEDERICH E. "Note-Takers vs. Non-Note-Takers: Who Makes More Errors?" *Journalism Quarterly* 46 (1969): 811–14.

ADLER, RUTH. *The Working Press.* New York: Putnam's Sons, 1966.

ALSOP, JOSEPH and STEWART. *The Reporter's Trade.* New York: Reynal, 1958. Chapter 1, "Trade Secrets."

ARLEN, MICHAEL J. "The Interview." The *New Yorker,* 10 November 1975, p. 141.

AUBRY, ARTHUR S., JR., and RUDOLPH R. CAPUTO. *Criminal Interrogation.* 2d ed. Springfield, Ill.: Charles C. Thomas, 1972.

AXELROD, MORRIS, and CHARLES F. CANNELL. "A Research Note on an Attempt to Predict Interviewer Effectiveness." *Public Opinion Quarterly* 23 (1959): 571–76.

"A Yellow School Bus. A Speeding Train. Then Sudden Tragedy . . ." *The Quill* June 1974, p. 22.

BABB, LAURA LONGLEY, ed. *Writing in Style.* Washington: The Washington Post, 1975.

BAHRICK, H. P., P. O. BAHRICK, and R. P. WITTLINGER. "Fifty Years of Memory for Names and Faces: A Cross-Sectional Approach." *Journal of Experimental Psychology* 104 (1975): 54–75.

BALINSKY, BENJAMIN, and RUTH BURGER. *The Executive Interview.* New York: Harper & Brothers, 1959.

BARKER, LARRY L. *Listening Behavior.* Englewood Cliffs, N. J.: Prentice-Hall, 1971.

BARTON, ALLEN E. "Asking the Embarrassing Question." *Public Opinion Quarterly* 22 (1958): 67–68. A welcome touch of tongue-in-cheek humor.

BARTON, MARY N., and MARION V. BELL. *Reference Books: A Brief Guide.* Baltimore: Enoch Pratt Free Library, 1970.

BECKER, THEODORE M., and PETER R. MEYERS. "Empathy and Bravado: Interviewing Reluctant Bureaucrats." *Public Opinion Quarterly* 38 (1974–75): 605–13.

BELL, EDWARD PRICE. "The Interview." *Journalism Bulletin* 1 (1925): 13–18.

156   REFERENCES, SOURCES, AND SELECTED BIBLIOGRAPHY

BENJAMIN, ALFRED. *The Helping Interview.* Boston: Houghton Mifflin, 1969.

BENNETT, ROGER E. "A Study of Variables in the Interviewing Process: The Naive Interviewer versus the Evasive News Source." Master's thesis, Ohio University, 1970.

BERNSTEIN, CARL, and BOB WOODWARD. *All the President's Men.* New York: Simon and Schuster, 1974. Account of investigative reporting techniques in the Watergate affair.

BINGHAM, WALTER VAN DYKE, and BRUCE VICTOR MOORE. *How to Interview.* 4th ed. New York: Harper & Row, 1959.

BIRDWHISTELL, RAY L. *Kinesics and Context.* Philadlephia: University of Pennsylvania Press, 1970. Body language.

BLACK, JAMES M. *How to Get Results from Interviewing.* New York: McGraw-Hill, 1970. Management oriented, but has good discussion of interviewing concepts in the first three chapters.

BLANCHARD, ROBERT O., ed. *Congress and the News Media.* New York: Hastings House, 1974. Several good essays on relationships between Congress and news representatives.

BOWEN, CATHERINE DRINKER. *Adventures of a Biographer.* Boston: Little, Brown, 1959.

———. *Biography: The Craft and the Calling.* Boston: Little, Brown, 1969.

BOWMAN, PIERRE. "A Budding TV Hostess with the Mostess?" *Honolulu Star-Bulletin,* 13 August 1974, sect. B, p. 10. About PBS's Jeanne Wolf.

BRADY, JOHN. *The Craft of Interviewing.* Cincinnati: Writer's Digest, 1976. Readable anecdotal treatment of interviewing, with tips from the pros.

———. "Gay Talese: An Exclusive Interview." part 2. *Writer's Digest,* February 1973, p. 26.

———. "Rex Reed." *Writer's Digest,* September 1973, p. 9.

BRIAN, DENIS. *Murderers and Other Friendly People.* New York: McGraw-Hill, 1973. Interviews with interviewers: Terkel, Talese, Salisbury, etc.

BROWN, JIM et al. "The Art of the Interview." *Folio,* February 1976, p. 63.

BRUSTEIN, ROBERT. "News Theater." The *New York Times Magazine,* 16 June 1974, p. 7.

BURGER, CHESTER. "How to Meet the Press." *Harvard Business Review,* July-August 1975, p. 62. How to be interviewed.

CANNELL, CHARLES F., and MORRIS AXELROD. "The Respondent Reports on the Interview." *American Journal of Sociology* 62 (1956): 177–81.

CANNELL, CHARLES F., and ROBERT L. KAHN. "Interviewing." In *Handbook of Social Psychology.* Edited by Gardner Lindzey and Elliott Aronson. 2d ed., vol. 2. Reading, Mass.: Addison-Wesley, 1968.

CAPLOW, THEODORE. "The Dynamics of Information Interviewing." *American Journal of Sociology* 62 (1956): 165–71.

CAPOTE, TRUMAN. *In Cold Blood.* New York: Random House, 1965.

CAVETT, DICK, and CHRISTOPHER PORTERFIELD. *Cavett.* New York: Harcourt Brace Jovanovich, 1974.

CHARNLEY, MITCHELL V. *Reporting.* 3d ed. New York: Holt, Rinehart and Winston, 1975. Chapters 8, 9, and 17.

CLIFFORD, JAMES L., ed. *Biography as an Art.* New York: Oxford University Press, 1962. Anthology of writings about biography.

————. *From Puzzles to Portraits: Problems of a Literary Biographer.* Chapel Hill: University of North Carolina Press, 1970.

COLES, ROBERT. *Children of Crisis: A Study of Courage and Fear.* Boston: Little, Brown, 1967. See Part I, "Method," for discussion of techniques of observation and participation.

CONVERSE, JEAN M., and HOWARD SCHUMAN. *Conversations at Random: Survey Research as Interviewers See It.* New York: Wiley, 1974.

COPPLE, NEALE. *Depth Reporting.* Englewood Cliffs, N. J.: Prentice-Hall, 1964.

CRONKITE, WALTER. *Eye on the World.* New York: Cowles Communications, 1971. Interesting broadcast interview snippets.

CROUSE, TIMOTHY. *The Boys On the Bus.* New York: Random House, 1973. Reporters in action in 1972 presidential campaign.

DALEY, ROBERT. "Super-Reporter: The Missing American Hero Turns Out to Be . . . Clark Kent." *New York,* 12 November 1973, p. 42. About investigative reporters.

DAVIS, FLORA. *Inside Intuition.* New York: McGraw-Hill, 1971. One of the more reasonable books on nonverbal communication.

DENNIS, EVERETTE E., and WILLIAM L. RIVERS. *Other Voices: The New Journalism in America.* San Francisco: Canfield Press, 1974.

DEXTER, LEWIS ANTHONY. *Elite and Specialized Interviewing.* Evanston, Ill.: Northwestern University Press, 1970. Especially useful for serious journalistic interviews.

DUNN, DELMER D. *Public Officials and the Press.* Reading, Mass.: Addison-Wesley, 1969. Legislative reporting in Wisconsin.

EDELHART, MIKE. "Tapping Yet Another Source: Telephone Research Without Hangups." *Writer's Digest,* June 1975, p. 20.

ELLIS, ALBERT. "Questionnaire versus Interview Methods in the Study of Human Love Relationships." *American Sociological Review* 12 (1947): 541–53.

FALLACI, ORIANA. *Interview With History.* New York: Liveright, 1976. One of several books containing interviews (and interview commentary) by this Italian journalist. Also see her *If the Sun Dies* (Atheneum, 1966), *The Limelighters* (Atheneum, 1967), and *The Egotists* (Regnery, 1968).

FANG, I. E. *Television News.* 2d ed. New York: Hastings House, 1972. Chapter 4, "Reporting."

FISCHER, JOHN. "Helping Hand for a Literary Upstart." *Harper's,* September 1963, p. 20.

FLEMING, KARL, and ANNE TAYLOR FLEMING. *The First Time.* New York: Simon and Schuster, 1975.

FONTAINE, ANDRÉ. *The Art of Writing Nonfiction.* New York: Thomas Y. Crowell, 1974. Chapters 3, 4, and 5.

GARRATY, JOHN A. "The Interrelations of Psychology and Biography." *Psychological Bulletin* 51 (1954): 569–82. Good description of uses of psychology in the writing of biography.

GARRETT, ANNETTE. *Interviewing: Its Principles and Methods.* 2d ed. New York: Family Service Association of America, 1972. Oriented to counseling, but good treatment of basics.

GILLELAND, LaRUE W. "Gilleland's GOSS Formula." *Journalism Educator* 26 (1971): 19–20. Also see *Editor & Publisher,* 18 September 1971, p. 54.

158

REFERENCES, SOURCES, AND SELECTED BIBLIOGRAPHY

GIVEN, JOHN L. *Making a Newspaper*. New York: Henry Holt, 1907.

GORDEN, RAYMOND L. *Interviewing: Strategy, Techniques and Tactics*. Homewood, Ill.: Dorsey Press, 1969.

GORA, JOEL M. *The Rights of Reporters*. New York: Avon, 1974. This ACLU handbook discusses legal aspects of reporter-interviewer's work, including protection of sources, access to records, confidentiality, invasion of privacy.

GRAVES, RALPH. "Visit to a Writer's Training Camp." *Life*, 7 July 1972, p. 3.

GREEN, MAURY. *Television News: Anatomy and Process*. Belmont, Calif.: Wadsworth, 1969. See part 3, "The Television Reporter."

GRIFFITH, THOMAS. *How True: A Skeptic's Guide to Believing the News*. Boston: Atlantic-Little Brown, 1974. Provocative commentary on methods of newsgathering.

GUNTHER, MAX. *Writing and Selling a Nonfiction Book*. Boston: The Writer, 1973. Chapters 6, 7, and 8.

GUSFIELD, JOSEPH R. "Field Work Reciprocities in Studying a Social Movement." In *Human Organization Research*. Edited by Richard N. Adams and Jack J. Preiss. Homewood, Ill.: Dorsey, 1960.

HAASE, RICHARD F., and DONALD T. TEPPER, JR. "Nonverbal Components of Empathic Communication." *Journal of Counseling Psychology* 19 (1972): 417–24.

HAGE, GEORGE S. et al. *New Strategies for Public Affairs Reporting*. Englewood Cliffs, N. J.: Prentice-Hall, 1976. A reporting text that concentrates on news coverage, not just writing.

HALL, EDWARD T. *The Hidden Dimension*. New York: Doubleday, 1966. Factors of space in human relationships.

HARMAN, JEANNE PERKINS. "Catch His Neurosis." In *Writer's Digest Handbook of Article Writing*. Edited by Frank A. Dickson. New York: Holt, Rinehart and Winston, 1968.

HARRALL, STEWART. *Keys to Successful Interviewing*. Norman: University of Oklahoma Press, 1954.

HAWKINS, WILLIAM J. "Pocket Tape Recorders." *Popular Science*, November 1975, p. 90.

HENTOFF, NAT et al. "The Art of the Interview." *(More)*, July 1975, p. 11.

HIGDON, HAL. "Interviewing the Famous, the Infamous, and the Non-Famous." Cincinnati: *1970 Writer's Yearbook*, p. 42.

HOHENBERG, JOHN. *The Professional Journalist*. 3d ed. New York: Holt, Rinehart and Winston, 1973.

HOWARD, JANE. "A Six-Year Literary Vigil." *Life*, 7 January 1966, p. 70. The story of Capote's *In Cold Blood*.

HULTENG, JOHN L. *The Messenger's Motives: Ethical Problems of the News Media*. Englewood Cliffs, N. J.: Prentice-Hall, 1976. Chapter 6, "Reporters and Sources."

HYMAN, HERBERT H. *Interviewing in Social Research*. Chicago: University of Chicago Press, 1954. Pioneering study of bias and error in social research interviewing.

INBAU, FRED E., and JOHN E. REID. *Criminal Interrogation and Confessions*. 2d ed. Baltimore: Williams & Wilkins, 1967.

INGLE, DARLENE. "Interviewing and the New Journalism: A Whole New Proposition." Unpublished research paper, School of Journalism, University of Oregon, 1973.

INGRAM, TIMOTHY. "Investigative Reporting: Is It Getting Too Sexy?" *The Washington Monthly*, April 1975. Good report on practices of investigative reporters and the pitfalls involved in their work.

IZARD, RALPH S., HUGH M. CULBERTSON, and DONALD A. LAMBERT. *Fundamentals of News Reporting*. 2d ed. Dubuque, Iowa: Kendall/Hunt, 1973. See Chapters 6, 7, and 8.

KAHN, ROBERT L., and CHARLES F. CANNELL. *The Dynamics of Interviewing*. New York: Wiley, 1957. Good discussion of psychological dynamics. Sample interview transcripts.

KILLENBERG, GEORGE M., and ROB ANDERSON. "Sources Are Persons: Teaching Interviewing As Dialogue." *Journalism Educator*, July 1976, p. 16.

KINCAID, HARRY V., and MARGARET BRIGHT. "Interviewing the Business Elite." *American Journal of Sociology* 63 (1957): 304–11.

KINSEY, ALFRED C., WARDELL B. POMEROY, and CLYDE E. MARTIN. *Sexual Behavior in the Human Male*. Philadelphia: W. B. Saunders, 1948. See Chapter 2, "Interviewing." Also see Kinsey et al., *Sexual Behavior in the Human Female*, 1953, Chapter 3, "Sources of Data."

KLEMESRUD, JUDY. "Oh, How She Loves to Get Up in the Morning . . ." The *New York Times*, 2 July 1967, sect. 2, p. 15. Barbara Walters on interviewing.

KLUCKHOLN, CLYDE. "The Personal Document in Anthropological Science." In *The Uses of Personal Documents in History, Anthropology, and Sociology*. New York: Social Science Research Council, Bulletin 53, 1945.

KRASNER, LEONARD. "Studies in the Conditioning of Verbal Behavior." *Psychological Bulletin* 55 (1958): 148–71.

KRIEGHBAUM, HILLIER, ed. *When Doctors Meet Reporters*. New York: New York University Press, 1957.

LAINE, MARGARET. "Broadcast Interviewing Handbook." Unpublished research paper, School of Journalism, University of Oregon, 1976.

LARSEN, OTTO N. "The Comparative Validity of Telephone and Face-to-Face Interviews in the Measurement of Message Diffusion from Leaflets." *American Sociological Review* 17 (1952): 471–76.

LATHAM, AARON. "An Evening in the Nude With Gay Talese." *New York*, 9 July 1973, p. 45.

LAWRENCE, GARY C., and DAVID L. GREY. "Subjective Inaccuracies in Local News Reporting." *Journalism Quarterly* 46 (1959): 753–57.

LEE, IRVING J. *How to Talk With People*. New York: Harper & Brothers, 1952.

LENZNOFF, MAURICE. "Interviewing Homosexuals." *American Journal of Sociology* 62 (1956): 202–204.

LIEBLING, A. J. "Goodbye, M.B.I." *New Yorker*, 7 February, 1948, p. 54.

———. *The Most of A. J. Liebling*. New York: Simon and Schuster, 1963. See "Interviewers," p. 156.

LIPPMANN, WALTER. *Public Opinion*. New York: Macmillan, 1922.

MAGEE, BRYAN. *The Television Interviewer*. London: MacDonald, 1966. Excellent account of experiences interviewing with the BBC.

MALIN, IRVING, ed. *Truman Capote's In Cold Blood: A Critical Handbook*. Belmont, Calif.: Wadsworth, 1968. Anthology of reviews and interviews including provocative critique of Capote's interviewing technique.

MALLOY, MICHAEL T. "Journalistic Ethics: Not Black, Not White, But . . . A Rainbow of Gray." *The National Observer*, 26 July 1975, p. 1.

MARCOSSON, ISAAC F. *Adventures in Interviewing*. New York: John Lane, 1919. A classic. Especially see Chapter 4, "The Art of Interviewing."

MARTIN, PETE. *Pete Martin Calls On* . . . New York: Simon and Schuster, 1962.

MATARRAZO, JOSEPH D., and ARTHUR N. WIENS. *The Interview: Research on Its Anatomy and Structure*. Chicago: Aldine-Atherton, 1972.

MAUROIS, ANDRÉ. *Aspects of Biography*. Translated by S. C. Roberts. New York: Appleton, 1929.

———. *Memoirs 1885–1967*. New York: Harper & Row, 1970. Chapter 36: "The Big Biographies."

MAXA, RUDY. "Dealing in Sweet Secrets: News Leaks as a Way of Doing Business." *The Quill*, September 1974, p. 18.

MAYER, MARTIN. *All You Know Is Facts*. New York: Harper & Row, 1969. See Preface.

McCOMBS, MAXWELL, DONALD LEWIS SHAW, and DAVID GREY. *Handbook of Reporting Methods*. Boston: Houghton Mifflin, 1976. Imaginative treatment of news and information gathering methods.

McCORMICK, MONA. *Who-What-When-Where-How-Why Made Easy*. Chicago: Quadrangle, 1971.

McHAM, DAVID. "The Authentic New Journalists." *The Quill*, September 1971, p. 9.

MEHRABIAN, ALBERT. *Nonverbal Communication*. Chicago: Aldine-Atherton, 1972.

———. *Silent Messages*. Belmont, Calif.: Wadsworth, 1971.

MERTON, ROBERT K., MARJORIE FISKE, and PATRICIA L. KENDALL. *The Focused Interveiw: A Manual of Problems and Procedures*. Glencoe, Ill.: Free Press, 1956.

MICHENER, JAMES A. *Kent State: What Happened and Why*. New York: Random House, 1971.

MILFORD, NANCY. "The Golden Dreams of Zelda Fitzgerald." *Harper's*, January 1969, p. 46. Interesting account of interviewing in the Old South for biographical work.

MILLER, S. M. "The Participant Observer and 'Over-Rapport.'" *American Sociological Review* 17 (1952): 97–99.

MOORE, WILLIAM T. *Dateline Chicago*. New York: Taplinger, 1973. Recounts "Front Page" journalism of the 20s and 30s.

MORGAN, THOMAS B. *Self-Creations: 13 Impersonalities*. New York: Holt, Rinehart and Winston, 1965. Interesting prefatory discussion of problems of coping with well-known personalities in magazine interviewing.

MORRIS, JIM R. "Newsmen's Interview Techniques and Attitudes Toward Interviewing." *Journalism Quarterly* 50 (1973): 539–42.

MULLIGAN, HUGH A. "Getting the Total Picture." In *Reporting: Writing from Front Row Seats*. Edited by Charles A. Grumich. New York: Simon and Schuster, 1971.

NEWQUIST, ROY, ed. *Counterpoint*. Chicago: Rand McNally, 1964.

NICHOLS, RALPH G., and LEONARD A. STEVENS. *Are You Listening?* New York: McGraw-Hill, 1957.

NILSSON, NILS GUNNAR. "The Origin of the Interview." *Journalism Quarterly* 48 (1971): 707–13.

PAYNE, STANLEY L. *The Art of Asking Questions.* Princeton, N. J.: Princeton University Press, 1951.

———. "Interviewer Memory Faults." *Public Opinion Quarterly* 13 (1949): 684–85.

PINKERTON, W. STEWART, JR. " 'New Journalism': Believe It or Not." In *The Press: A Critical Look from the Inside.* Edited by A. Kent MacDougall. Princeton, N. J.: Dow Jones, 1972.

PLIMPTON, GEORGE. "The Story Behind a Nonfiction Novel." The *New York Times Book Review,* 16 January 1966, p. 38.

POLANSKY, NORMAN A. *Ego Psychology and Communication.* Chicago: Aldine, 1971.

POMEROY, WARDELL B. *Dr. Kinsey and the Institute for Sex Research.* New York: Harper & Row, 1972. Chapter 7, "Interviewing."

POOL, ITHIEL DE SOLA. "A Critique of the 20th Anniversary Issue." *Public Opinion Quarterly* 21 (1957): 190–98. "Every interview is an interpersonal drama with a developing plot."

POPE, BENJAMIN, and ARON W. SIEGMAN. "Interviewer Warmth in Relation to Interviewee Verbal Behavior." *Journal of Consulting and Clinical Psychology* 32 (1968): 558–95.

———, and THOMAS BLASS. "Anxiety and Speech in the Initial Interview." *Journal of Consulting and Clinical Psychology* 35 (1970): 233–38.

POWERS, THOMAS. *Diana: The Making of a Terrorist.* Boston: Houghton Mifflin, 1971.

QUAY, HERBERT. "The Effect of Verbal Reinforcement on the Recall of Early Memories." *Journal of Abnormal and Social Psychology* 59 (1959): 254–57.

REIK, THEODOR. *The Compulsion to Confess.* New York: Farrar, Straus and Cudahy, 1959.

———. *Listening With the Third Ear.* New York: Farrar, Straus, 1952.

RICE, STUART A. "Contagious Bias in the Interview." *American Journal of Sociology* 35 (1929): 420–23.

RICHARDSON, STEPHEN A., BARBARA SNELL DOHRENWEND, and DAVID KLEIN. *Interviewing: Its Forms and Functions.* New York: Basic Books, 1965. Basic and thorough treatise on interviewing.

RILEY, SAM G., and JOEL M. WIESSLER. "Privacy: the Reporter and Telephone and Tape Recorder." *Journalism Quarterly* 51 (1974): 511–15.

RIVERS, WILLIAM L. *The Adversaries.* Boston: Beacon Press, 1970. Relationship of reporters with government sources.

———. *Finding Facts: Interviewing, Observing, Using Reference Sources.* Englewood Cliffs, N. J.: Prentice-Hall, 1975.

ROBINSON, JAMES A. "Survey Interviewing Among Members of Congress." *Public Opinion Quarterly* 24 (1960): 127–38.

ROBINSON, LEONARD WALLACE et al. "The New Journalism." *Writer's Digest,* January 1970, p. 32. Interview with Harold Hayes, Gay Talese, and Tom Wolfe.

ROGERS, CARL R., and F. J. ROETHLISBERGER. "Barriers and Gateways to Communication." *Harvard Business Review,* July-August 1952, p. 46.

ROGERS, CARL R. *Client-Centered Therapy.* Boston: Houghton Mifflin, 1951.

———. *Counseling and Psychotherapy.* Boston: Houghton Mifflin, 1942.

ROSE, CAMILLE DAVIED. *How to Write Successful Magazine Articles.* Boston: The Writer, 1967. Chapters 4 and 5, research and interviewing.

ROSS, LILLIAN. *Reporting.* New York: Simon and Schuster, 1964.

SANFORD, DAVID. "The Lady of the Tapes." *Esquire,* June 1975, p. 102. Good portrait of Oriana Fallaci, Italian journalist known for her provocative interviews.

SCHAPPER, BEATRICE, ed. *Writing the Magazine Article from Idea to Printed Page.* Cincinnati: Writer's Digest, 1970. Eight case histories of published magazine articles.

SHALIT, GENE. "The Woman You Never See on TV." *Ladies' Home Journal,* November 1975, p. 98. Barbara Walters.

SHERWOOD, HUGH C. *The Journalistic Interview.* 2d ed. New York: Harper & Row, 1972.

SIGAL, LEON V. *Reporters and Officials.* Lexington, Mass.: Heath, 1973.

SPIKOL, ART. "Taping and Tapping." *Writer's Digest,* April 1976, p. 46. Legal aspects of taping telephone conversations.

STEFFENS, LINCOLN. *The Autobiography of Lincoln Steffens.* New York: Harcourt, Brace, 1931.

STEIN, M. L. *When Presidents Meet the Press.* New York: Julian Messner, 1969.

STEWART, CHARLES J., and WILLIAM B. CASH. *Interviewing: Principles and Practices.* Dubuque, Iowa: Wm. C. Brown, 1974.

TALESE, GAY. "Joe Louis: The King as a Middle Aged Man." *Esquire,* June 1962, p. 92.

TERKEL, STUDS. *Division Street: America.* New York: Pantheon, 1967. See "Prefatory Notes."

———. *Hard Times: An Oral History of the Great Depression.* New York: Pantheon, 1970.

———. *Working: People Talk About What They Do All Day and How They Feel About What They Do.* New York: Pantheon, 1974. See "Introduction."

TOKHEIM, MARY. "Bizarre Behavior in the Interview." *Public Opinion Quarterly* 38 (1974): 462–63.

TRENTO, JOSEPH. "The Long Distance Interview." *Writer's Digest,* July 1972. Interviewing by phone and mail.

TYRREL, ROBERT. *The Work of the Television Journalist.* New York: Hastings House, 1972. Chapters 8 and 9 on reporting and interviewing for the BBC.

WALTERS, BARBARA. *How to Talk With Practically Anybody About Practically Anything.* Garden City, N. Y.: Doubleday, 1970.

WAX, ROSALIE HANKEY. "Twelve Years Later: An Analysis of Field Experience." *American Journal of Sociology* 63 (1957): 133–42.

WEAVER, CARL H. *Human Listening.* New York: Bobbs-Merrill, 1972.

WEBB, EUGENE J., and JERRY R. SALANCIK. *The Interview or The Only Wheel in Town.* Austin, Texas: The Association for Education in Journalism. Journalism Monographs No. 2, November 1966. An eye-opener for journalistic interviewers.

WEBB, EUGENE J. et al. *Unobtrusive Measures: Nonreactive Research in the Social Sciences.* Chicago: Rand McNally, 1966. A delightful book on methods of systematic observation, valuable for journalists.

WEBER, RONALD, ed. *The Reporter as Artist.* New York: Hastings House, 1974. Good compendium of essays about new journalism by Tom Wolfe, Dan Wakefield, George Plimpton, and others.

WEITZ, SHIRLEY, ed. *Nonverbal Communication.* New York: Oxford University Press, 1974.

WELLMAN, FRANCIS L. *The Art of Cross-Examination.* 4th ed. New York: Macmillan, 1936.

WHITMAN, ALDEN. *The Obituary Book.* New York: Stein and Day, 1970. See "The Art of the Obituary," p. 7.

WHYTE, WILLIAM FOOTE. "Interviewing in Field Research." In *Human Organization Research.* Edited by Richard N. Adams and Jack J. Preiss. Homewood, Ill.: Dorsey Press, 1960.

WIGGINTON, ELIOT, ed. *The Foxfire Book.* Garden City, N. Y.: Doubleday, 1972. A delightful collection of interviews of Georgia hill country folks by members of a high school class. See also *Foxfire 2* and *Foxfire 3.*

WOLF, LINDA M. *Anthropological Interviewing in Chicago.* Chicago: Department of Anthropology, University of Chicago, 1964. Many parallels with journalistic interviewing.

WOLFE, TOM. "The Birth of 'The New Journalism'; Eyewitness Report by Tom Wolfe." *New York,* 14 February 1972, p. 1.

———. *The New Journalism.* New York: Harper and Row, 1973. Anthology with prefatory chapter by Wolfe on nature of the new journalism.

———. "The New Journalism." *The Bulletin* of the American Society of Newspaper Editors, September 1970, p. 1.

———. "Why They Aren't Writing the Great American Novel Anymore." *Esquire* December 1972, p. 152.

ZOLOTOW, MAURICE. "Studying a Subject." In *Writer's Digest Handbook of Article Writing.* Edited by Frank A. Dickson. New York: Holt, Rinehart and Winston, 1968.

ZUCKERMAN, HARRIET. "Interviewing an Ultra-Elite." *Public Opinion Quarterly* 36 (1972): 159–75.

ZUNIN, LEONARD, and NATALIE B. ZUNIN. *Contact: The First Four Minutes.* Los Angeles: Nash, 1972. Psychological dynamics of first meetings between strangers.

Index

Accuracy in interviewing, 30–32, 137
Ad-libbing questions (See Probes)
Adventures in Interviewing, 52, 131
Adventures of a Biographer, 117
Afterthoughts, at end of interview, 21
Agencies as news sources, 81, 83
Agriculture news beat, 80
Aimlessness in interviewing, 4, 7, 139–44
(See also Faults)
All-purpose questions (See Universal questions)
Alsop, Joseph, 76–77
Alsop, Stewart, 76–77
American City, 86
American Society of Newspaper Editors, 107
Anatomy of interview (See Structure of interview)
Anecdotes, 45–49, 152
defined, 45
importance, 152
obtaining, 46, 47–49
written sample, 49
Anonymous sources, 135, 136 (See also Sources)
Answers
anticipating them, 59–60
basis for futher questions, 5, 16, 41–42, 45
boring, 138
credibility, 132–33
evasive, 134
hostile, 131
"no comment," 27, 130, 153
nonstop, 52, 62, 97–98
off the record, 135–36, 153
platitudinous, 5
unpredicted, 2, 4, 18, 61–63
Antagonistic questions (See confrontation tactics)
Appearance, 5

Appointment for interview, 17–18, 60, 129–31
Arcaro, Eddie, 52–53
Are You Listening?, 29
Argumentation, by interviewer, 44–45
Articles, nonfiction, 66–68
Art of Asking Questions, The, 35
Art of Writing Nonfiction, The, 73
Ashland Daily Tidings, 150
Asking, as "strength," 2
Associated Press, 76, 113, 123
Authority
in quotes, 44
as "truth," 133
Axelrod, Morris, 30

Babb, Laura Longley, 65
Babbs, Ken, 119
Bacon, Francis, 119
Bahrick, H. P., 133
Baker, Ann, 150–54
Balinsky, Benjamin, 26
Bank robber, telephone interview, 24
Bardot, Brigitte, 105
Barton, Mary N., 57
Beats (See News beats)
Being interviewed, 17–18, 139–40
Bell, Edward Price, 123
Bell, Marion V., 57
Bellamy, Ron, 131
Benny, Jack, 115
Berkeley student rebellion, 133
Bernstein, Carl, 136
Better Homes & Gardens, 77
Bias, of interviewer, 30–31, 131
Biographical interviews, 105, 115–17 (See also Personality interviews)
Biography Index, 56
Bits and pieces (See Fragmented information)
Black interviewers, 30–31

Bluffing, 136 (*See also* Ethics)
Body language (*See* Nonverbal communi-
    cation)
"Bomb" questions, 19–20
    on broadcast, 97
Bonanno, Bill, 113–14
Book Beat, 98
Book Review Index, 57
Boorish interviewing, 26, 27 (*See also* Con-
    frontation tactics)
Boredom
    in interviewer, 35
    in respondent, 138
Boswell, James, 119
Bowen, Catherine Drinker, 117
Brady, John, 104
Breaking the ice, 11–12, 19, 35–36, 60
Brian, Denis, 119
Broadcast interviewing, 93–102
    defined, 93–95, 99
    different from print, 93–95
    like drifting a river, 93, 100
    extended, 95–98
    interruptions, 97–98
    microphone "swordplay," 99–100
    opening questions, 97
    performing, 95, 98, 100–102
    qualities of interviewer, 100
    questioning techniques, 96–98
    quickie, 99–100
    rehearsal, 97
    rapport, 95, 100–102
    selection of guest, 96
    technical problems, 95, 96, 99
    time cues, 95, 98, 102
"Broadcast Interviewing Handbook," 94n
Brustein, Robert, 26
Buckley, William F., 96
Bulletin of the ASNE, 107
Bureaucracy, interviewing in, 54–55, 81–
    83 (*See also* News beats)
Bureaucrats as respondents, 10, 81–82, 136,
    153–54
Burger, Ruth, 26
Burton, Richard, 23
Business news beat, 80
Business Periodical Index, 56

Campus demonstrations, 81, 133
Candor (*See also* Truth)
    in conceptual questions, 40
    in personality interviews, 118
    in respondent, 7, 132
Cannell, Charles F., 30
"Can this Marriage Be Saved?" 111
Capote, Truman, 24, 77, 105, 106, 114, 118,
    119, 123
Carelessness, in appearance, 5
Case history interview, 111–12
Cassette recorder (*See* Tape recorders)
Cavett, Dick, 94, 98
CBS Morning News, 23
Celebrity interviews, 104–105, 106, 109–11,
    115 (*See also* Personality interviews)
Challenges, as interview technique, 45

Change, through listening, 29–30
Character assessment, in interview plan-
    ning, 57
Chicago, 108
Christian Science Monitor Index, 57
Chronicle of Higher Education, 86, 89
Chronological questions, 36–37
Chronology, as interview structure, 61
Chubbock, Christine, 65
Church, Sen. Frank, 99
Churchill, Winston, 117
Circumlocution, in questions, 6
City services news beat, 79
Class exercises, 144–49
Clichés, journalistic, 7, 10, 12–13, 138
Clippings, for research, 55–56
Closing the interview, 20
Clothes, 5
Clues
    in anecdote soliciting, 47
    in questioning, 15–16, 49–50, 52, 117–18
Coaches as respondents, 12
Coffee cup reporting, 83, 88
Colorado, 133
Colored questions, 35, 44 (*See also* Ques-
    tions)
Communication
    of feelings, 32, 94
    first meetings, 19, 35–36
    free flow of, 26, 28–30
    nonverbal, 31, 32–33
    personal, 28–30
Community relations officer, 81–82, 83–85
Composites, 112 (*See also* New journalism)
"Compulsion to confess," 24
Conceptually defining questions, 40–41
Concluding the interview, 20–21
"Conditioning" for interview, 51–52
Confidentiality, 71–72, 112
    of tapes, 126
Confrontation tactics
    bargaining, 88
    "don't quote me," 153
    hardline approach, 26–27
    in investigative reporting, 53–54
    in newsgathering, 151
    and "over-rapport," 71
    power of press, 31–32, 88
    sensitive questions, 26–27, 30
Contact: The First Four Minutes, 19
Control of interview (*See* Structure; Pac-
    ing)
Conversation, 10 (*See also* Rapport)
Convoluted questions, 6
Copple, Neale, 70
Corroboration, 132, 136 (*See also* Truth)
County news beat, 79
Courts news beat, 79
Coverup tactics, 27, 40 (*See also* Evasive-
    ness)
Creative Interview
    defined, 10
    "discovered," 15–16
    in personality interviewing, 117–18
    sample transcript, 11–16

Creative questions, 49–50
Credibility, 132–33
Crime Control Act 1973, 56
Crime task force, 61–62
Criminals, as respondents, 24–26, 103
Critical questions, 26
Crockett, Ken, 96, 97
Cromie, Robert, 98
Cronkite, Walter, 25n
Cumulative Book Index, 57
Curiosity
   childlike, 1, 2
   as interview structure, 61
   as motivation, 24

Deceit (*See also* Ethics)
   by interviewer, 29, 85, 139
   by respondent, 77
"Defining before seeing," 6, 66
Defoe, Daniel, 66
Depth Reporting, 70, 80–81
Depth Reporting, 70
Detail
   in anecdotes, 47
   in case history, 111, 112
   for dramatic effect, 69–70
   recalled in memory, 133–34
   saturation reporting, 107, 118
   in scenes, 65
Devil's advocacy, 44–45
Discipline, in conversation, 124
Division Street: America, 9
Documents
   in interviewing, 21, 57
   library research, 55–57
   in memory recall, 134
   on news beats, 87
   in news coverage, 82
Dogmatic reporters, 6 (*See also* Listening)
Dorian Gray, 44
Dramatizing, 68–70
Dress, 5
"Dumb question," 34

Education Index, 56
Education for interviewing
   by being interviewed, 139–40
   need, 151
   exercises, 144–49
Education news beat, 80
Ego reinforcement
   after "bomb," 20
   interviewer's subjugated, 30, 32
   in opening questions, 37, 131
Elected officials as respondents, 81, 153
Electric Kool-Aid Acid Test, 106, 118
Ellis, Albert, 31
Embarrassing questions (*See* Sensitive questions)
Emergency services news beat, 79
Empathy, 23–25 (*See also* Rapport)
Ending the interview, 20–21
Entertainment news beat, 80
Error in interview (*See* Bias; Accuracy)
Esquire, 115–16
Essay, in nonfiction, 67–68

Ethics
   anonymous sources, 135–36
   bargaining, 88
   bluffing, 136
   colored questions, 35, 44
   in evasiveness, 134
   flattery, 129, 130
   in getting interview, 129–30
   leading questions, 44
   new candor, 136
   not for attribution, 135
   off the record, 135–36, 153
   ploys, 129–30
   power of the press, 31–32, 88
   pre-publication review, 136–37
   subterfuges, 129–30
Etiquette in interview, 35
Eugene, Oregon, 130
Eugene Register-Guard, 150–54 *passim*
Evasiveness, 134
Exchange of information, 10, 74–75
   in creative interview, 10, 15–16
Executive Interview, The, 26
Exercises for classes, 144–49
Eye on the World, 25n

Faces, 106
Factions among respondents, 71
Factual questions, 38–39
Factual report, in nonfiction, 67
Fallaci, Oriana, 38
Fang, I. E., 94–95
Faults of interviewing
   aimlessness, 4, 7, 139–44
   bias, 30–31, 131
   convoluted questions, 6
   defining before seeing, 6, 66
   dogmatism, 6
   filibustering, 7
   indirection, 8, 20, 131
   insensitivity, 6, 26–27, 31–32
   laziness, 7
   listening failures, 2, 6, 7, 125
   in sample transcript, 141–43
      discussed, 143–44
   selfconsciousness, 3, 4
   unpreparedness, 4–5, 90–92
   vagueness, 5
Feature interview, 109–11 (*See also* Personality interview)
Federal news beat, 80
Feelings, communicated, 32
   in broadcast, 94
Female police officers (*See* Policewomen)
"File" of interview information, 147, 150–54
Filibustering, 7
Filter questions, 38
First meeting with respondent, 11–12, 19, 35–36
First Time, The, 136
Fischer, John, 106
Fishing for news, 75, 76, 83–85
Flattery, 129, 130
Flemming, Karl, 69–70
Follow questions (*See* Probe questions)

Fontaine, André, 73
"Fool for five minutes," proverb, 2
"Foolproof questions," 23 (*See also* Universal questions)
Foxfire Book, The, 148
Fragmented information, 72, 149
Franks, Lucinda, 107
Freeman, Vance, 151
Friendly approach to interviewing, 2–3 (*See also* Rapport)
Front Page, 81
Funnel questions, 38, 59
Future book, 87

Garbo, Greta, 23
Getting interview appointment, 17–18, 60, 129–31
Gilleland, LaRue, 40–41
Given, John L., 77, 78
Gold mining, like interviewing, 19, 47–49
GOSS formula, 40–41, 85
Government Periodicals Index, 57
Grand Canyon, 43
Griffith, Thomas, 26

Hailey, Arthur, 77, 135
Hall, Edward T., 32–33
Harassment (*See* Ethics)
Hardline interviewing, 26–27 (*See also* Ethics)
Hard Times, 135, 147
Harper's, 106
Harrall, Stewart, 76
Harvard Business Review, 28
Hawaii, 4, 80
Hearst, Patricia, 76, 103
Hemingway, Ernest, 114
Hepburn, Katharine, 110–11
Hickock, Richard, 24
Hidden Dimension, The, 32–33
Hightower, John M., 76
"Hm-mmm," as interview response, 31, 45
in broadcast, 98
Hohenberg, John, 23, 30
Holcomb, Kansas, 77
Holmes, Sherlock, 66
Homework (*See* Preparation)
Honolulu, 5, 126
Honor Thy Father, 113
Horne, Peter, 57
Hostility
by interviewer, 23, 131
by respondent, 3, 37–38
on TV, 2, 68, 94, 99
How to Talk with People, 28
How to Talk with Practically Anybody about Practically Anything, 37
How True: A Skeptic's Guide to Believing the News, 26
Huie, William Bradford, 20
Humanistic reporting, 106
Humanities Index, 56
Human touches, 68 (*See also* Personality interviewing)
Humor
in questions, 36, 38

Humor (*cont.*)
in quotations, 43, 68
Humphrey, Hubert, 51
Hunches in interviewing, 47–49, 52, 85 (*See also* Clues)
Huston, John, 114
Hypothetical questions, 49–50 (*See also* Creative questions)

Icebreaker questions, 11–12, 19, 35–36, 60
Idiosyncracies
in personality interviewing, 68, 107
in quotes, 42–44
in respondents, 57–58, 68, 117, 120
Image problem, 104–5, 115
Incidents (*See* Anecdotes)
In Cold Blood, 24, 77, 105, 106, 114, 123
Indian legends, 71
Indians as respondents, 71
Indirection in interviewing, 8, 20, 131
Inexperienced interviewers, 139–44
transcript, 141–43
Inexperienced respondents, 12, 154
Informants, 72 (*See also* Sources; Tips and tipsters)
Ingle, Darlene, 118–19
In-house interviewing (*See* Interviewing, in organizations)
Insensitivity
in interviewer, 6, 26–27, 31–32
in respondent, 26
Intellectuals, as respondents, 154
Intensity in interviews, 98
Interior monologue, 65–66
Interpretative reporting, 31–32 (*See also* Depth reporting; New journalism)
Interrogation, 72
Interrupting
in broadcast, 97–98
Interview, the
anatomy (*See* Stages of the interview)
bias, 30–31, 131
creative, 10, 15–16, 117–18
defined, 10
as data processing, 9
"deceptively easy," 139–40
defined, 9–10
file, 147, 150–54
like floating a river, 93, 100
like goldmining, 19, 47–49
importance of, 150
as learning experience, 72
as multidimensional human contact, 9–10
performance, 95, 98, 100–102, 104
as "poker game," 136
purpose, 4, 16, 53–55
respondent enjoyment, 24, 30
like salesmanship, 52
structure, 11, 16–21, 60–62
like waltzing to music, 117
Interviewee (*See* Respondent)
Interviewers, journalistic, quoted
Bell, Edward Price, 123
Bellamy, Ron, 131
Bernstein, Carl, 136

Interviewers (cont.)
  Bowen, Catherine Drinker, 117
  Capote, Truman, 24, 77, 105, 106, 114,
    118, 119, 123
  Cavett, Dick, 98
  Crockett, Ken, 96, 97
  Cromie, Robert, 98
  Fallaci, Oriana, 38
  Fontaine, André, 73
  Hightower, John M., 76
  Johnson, Janis, 148, 150–54
  Krauss, Bob, 77–78
  Kucera, Kathy, 24
  Laine, Margaret, 93–100 passim, 140–44
  Liebling, A. J., 24, 52–53, 75, 138
  Lucas, Jim G., 76
  McGee, Frank, 98
  Magarrell, Jack, 89
  Marcosson, Isaac, 52, 131
  Martin, Pete, 110, 120–21
  Meryman, Richard, 51–52
  Mich, Dan, 17
  Miller, Floyd, 70
  Morgan, Thomas B., 104
  Quinn, Sally, 23, 65
  Reed, Rex, 104
  Ross, Lillian, 114
  Royko, Mike, 23
  Spencer, Murlin, 123
  Steffens, Lincoln, 62
  Talese, Gay, 113–14, 115–16, 118
  Terkel, Studs, 9–10, 29, 102, 104, 119,
    135, 147, 148
  Thoele, Mike, 134
  Wallace, Mike, 94, 98
  Walters, Barbara, 23, 37, 98
  Wissbeck, Larry, 94, 96
  Wolf, Jeanne, 98, 133
  Wolfe, Tom, 106–7, 115, 118, 119
  Woodward, Bob, 136
  Zolotow, Maurice, 105
Interviewers, as respondents, 22–23
Interviewer silence, 4, 34, 45, 89–90
Interviewing
  accuracy, 30–32, 137
  appointment request, 17–18, 60, 129–31
  apprehension of students, 1, 2, 3
  for broadcast, 93–102
  concluding, 20–21
  for detail, 47, 107, 111, 112, 118, 133–134
  dramatizing, 68–70
  education for, 151
  ending, 20–21
  getting appointment, 17–18, 60, 129–31
  multiple-interview projects, 64–74
  in new journalism, 65–66, 106–7, 113–14,
    115–16, 118–19
  observation, 73–74, 113, 114
  in organizations
    key people, 54, 71
    manipulators, 72
    objectivity, 71–72
    observation, 73–74
    trading information, 72–73
    voluntary informants, 72
  pacing, 19, 124, 133 (See also Structure)

Interviewing (cont.)
  perception, 115–116
  personality, 103–21
  planning, 18
  preparation, 4–5, 16, 17, 18, 51–53, 90–
    92, 96–97
  rapport, 19, 23–25, 26–27, 28–30, 38, 125–
    26
  setting, 11, 32–33, 95
  by telephone, 83–85, 88–90, 129, 151
  transcripts, sample, 11–16, 47–49, 83–85,
    141–43
  analyzed, 16, 143–44
  unpreparednes, 4–5, 90–92
  by VD investigator, 141–43
"Interviewing and the New Journalism,"
    119n
Interview or the Only Wheel in Town,
    The, 30
"Interview Report: Ann Baker," 150n
Interview seminar, 140, 144
In the Know, 106
Intuition, interview topic, 73
Involvement, through listening, 29
Issues in Police Administration, 57

Jackrabbits, in Nevada, 68
Jackson, Reggie, 131
James, William, 52
Janitors, as sources, 83
Jargon
  in bureaucracies, 75
  in quotes, 43
Jeanne Wolf With . . . , 98
Jewish interviewer, 31
Johnson, Janis, 148, 150–54
Journalistic "street walkers," 82
Journalists as respondents, 23
Kansas, 24

Kaye, Danny, 120–21
Kesey, Ken, 118–19
Key people, 54, 71 (See also Soures; Re-
    spondents)
Keys to Successful Interviewing, 76
Kennan, George, 28
Kent State shooting, 72
KGW-TV, 94
King, Alan, 23
Kinsey, Dr. Alfred, 22–23
Kipling, Rudyard, 38–39
Kissinger, Henry, 96
Klemesrud, Judy, 23
Kluckholn, Clyde, 73
Krauss, Bob, 77–78
Kucera, Kathy, 24
Ku Klux Klan, 43

Ladies' Home Journal, 56, 98, 110, 111
Laine, Margaret, 93–100 passim, 140–44
La Rochefoucauld, François duc de, 44
Law & Order, 86
Laziness, 7
Lee, Irving, 28
Legwork, 147
Lensnoff, Maurice, 71

Leverage in interviewing, 88 (*See also* Ethics)
Levy, Alan, 110
Liberace, 23
Library
  card catalog, 57
  city, 56–57
  newspaper, 55–56
Liebling, A. J., 24, 52–53, 75, 138
Life, 51, 52
Lippmann, Walter, 78
Listening
  brings change, 29–30
  brings involvement, 29
  faults, 2, 6, 7, 125
  nonjudgmental, 24, 28–29, 131
  restating respondent's comment, 28
  "with third ear," 116–17
  while taping, 125–26
  while typing, 125
Listening with the Third Ear, 116–17
Literary effect, 69 (*See also* New journalism)
Literary techniques (*See* New journalism; Anecdotes; Dramatizing)
Look, 17
Long-distance interviewing (*See* Telephone interviewing)
Loren, Sophia, 110
Los Angeles, 116
Louis, Joe, 116
Love relationships, study, 31
Lucas, Jim, 76
Luck in interviewing, 52
Lying
  checking, 132–33
  discouraging, 28–29
  discovering, 22–23, 28–29

McCall's, 110
McGee, Frank, 98
Mafia, observing, 113–14
Magarrell, Jack, 89
Magazine interviewing, 53, 67, 89
Mahar, Ted, 110–11
Making a Newspaper, 77
Malloy, Michael T., 23
Manipulators
  as informants, 72
  journalistic street walkers, 82
  "media freak," 137
Marcosson, Isaac F., 52, 131
Martin, Pete, 110, 120–21
Maryland, 64
Maurois, André, 105
"Media freak," 137
Meeting the respondent, 11–12, 19, 35–36
Meet the Press, 2, 68, 94
Mehrabian, Albert, 32
Memory problems
  interviewer's, 123, 124
  respondent's, 133–134
Merry Pranksters, 118–19
Meryman, Richard, 51–52
"Metzler's Law," 47n
Mich, Dan, 17

Michener, James, 72
Middleage respondents, 13
"Milestones" as news, 79
Miller, Floyd, 70
Miller, S. M., 71
Mini-recorder (*See* Tape recorders)
Misquotation (*See* Quotations)
Miss Oregon, 117
Moneychangers, The, 77
Moore, Mary Tyler, 110
(MORE), 23
Morgan, Thomas B., 104–5
Most of A. J. Liebling, The, 24, 53
Multiple interviews, 64–74
  conflicting statements, 64–65
  and depth reporting, 70–71
  detail, 65, 69–70
  dramatizing, 68–70
  key people, 71
  learning progression, 72
  and new journalism, 65–66
  in nonfiction articles, 66–68
  objectivity, 71–72
  observation, 73–74
  trading information, 72–73
Munich, Germany, 130
Murderers and Other Friendly People, 119
Mystery
  created by tough questions, 27
  literary suspense, 69

Names, use of, 36
Narrative, interviewing for, 114 (*See also* Saturation reporting; New journalism)
Nashville, 108
National Observer, 23
Nervousness (*See* Selfconsciousness)
Nestvold, Karl, 99
Nevada, 68
New journalism
  participant-observer, 113–14
  saturation reporting, 106–7, 118–19
  scenes dramatized, 115–16
  trend toward, 65–66, 106–7
Newnham, Blaine, 130–31
News
  defined, 77–79
  "milestones," 79
  perceived, 78
  problems in getting, 75–76
News beats, 75–92
  agency contact, 81–83
  defined, 77–79
  getting started, 81–88
  listed, 79–80
  by phone, 88–90
  problems, 75–77
  sources, 76, 83–85, 132, 135, 136
  universal questions, 85–86, 91
News clippings, for research, 55–56
News conference, 27, 134–35
  by President Nixon, 26
Newspaper library, 55–56
News reporting (*See* Reporting)
News sources (*See* Sources)

"News Theater," 26
News watchers, 77–78 (See also News Beats)
Newsweek, 69, 106, 108
New York, 112
New York City, 56, 73, 116
New Yorker, 52, 75, 112
New York Times, 23
New York Times Index, 56
New York Times Magazine, 56
Nichols, Ralph, 29, 30
Nixon, Richard M., 26
"No comment," 27, 130, 153 (See also Hostility; Evasiveness)
Nonfiction article
  defined, 66–68
  essay, as part, 67–68
  factual report, as part, 67
  short story, as part, 68
Nonjudgmental listening, 24, 28–29, 131
Nonstop talkers, 52, 62, 97–98
Nonthematic interview, 110–11
Nonverbal communication, 31, 32–33, 124
Nonverbal cues, 15
Nonverbal rewards, 31
Nose for news (See News, defined)
Not for attribution, 135 (See also Ethics)
Notes on interview (See Interview, file)
Notetaking, 7, 122–25, 151
  accuracy, 123
  and listening, 7, 122, 123
  for quotes, 124
  relying on memory, 123, 124, 151
  shorthand, 123, 124
  from tape recorder, 126–27
  on typewriter, 125, 151
  on video display terminal, 125
Numerically defining questions, 39–40
"Nutty people," as respondents, 154
Nyack, New York, 70

Obituary Book, The, 105
Objectivity, 15–16, 71–72 (See also Bias)
Observation, 55
  for detail, 73–74
  informal, 55, 74–75
  in Mafia, 113–14
  in new journalism, 113–14
  of scenes, 65, 113–14, 115–16
Off the record, 135–36, 153 (See also Ethics)
Ohio Wesleyan University, 133
Oklahoma, 140
Oklahoma City, 140
Olympics, 130, 131
Onassis, Aristotle, 37
Ontario, California, 108
Opening questions
  in broadcast, 97
  first moves, 36
  icebreakers, 11–12, 19, 35, 60
Opie Dildock Pass, 66
Oral history interviewing, 2
Oregon, 4, 24, 43, 90, 134
  rain, 130
Oregonian, The, 110
Organization of interview (See Structure of interview)

Organizations, interviewing in (See Interviewing, in organizations)
Oriental interviewer, 30–31
Oughton, Diana, 107
Overheard conversations, 55, 73
"Over-rapport," 71–72

Pacing the interview, 19, 124, 133 (See also Structure of interview)
PAIS Index, 56
Paranoia, in respondent, 46
Parents', 74
Participant-Observer (See Observation)
Payne, Stanley, 35
People, 106, 109
Peoria, Illinois, 56
Perception in interviewing, 6, 78, 115–16
Permissiveness (See Rapport)
Pershing, Gen. John J., 52
Personality interview, 103–21
  case history, 111–12
  celebrities, 104–5, 106, 109–11, 115
  feature, 109–11
  human touches, 120–21
  interviewing people close to subject, 13–14, 51, 58
  key person, as literary device, 68–69
  as life to dull issues, 107–8
  problems, 103–5
  profile, 112–14
  psychology, 104–5, 114–16
  questions, 119–20
  sidebar, 108–9
  sketch, 109
  themes, 67, 110, 113
  types, 107–114
  uses, 103, 105–7
"Pete Martin Calls On. . . ," 110
Pete Martin Calls On. . . , 120–21
Philadelphia, 53
Phone (See Telephone)
Phoning for appointment (See Getting interview appointment)
Phrasing questions, 58–59
Picture, 114
Planning an interview (See Strategy of interview)
Playboy, 110
Playboy Index, 56
Pleasure in being interviewed, 11, 24, 30
Ploys, 130 (See also Ethics)
Pocket tape recorder (See Tape recorders)
Police chief, hypothetical interview, 53–63
Police Foundation, 56, 57, 58, 59
Policewoman, 57
Policewomen, hypothetical interview topic, 53–63, 67, 68–70
Policewomen on Patrol: A Final Report, 57
Politics news beat, 80
Portable tape recorder (See Tape recorders)
Postinterview questionnaire, 145
Power of press, 31–32, 88 (See also Ethics)
Powers, Thomas, 107
Practice interviews, 144–49
  for newswriting class, 148–49

Practice interviews (*cont.*)
  questionnaires, 145
  role playing, 144, 148–49
Prefontaine, Steve, 130–31
Preinterview planning (*See* Strategy of interview)
Preinterview questionnaire, 145
Preinterview research (*See* Strategy of interview)
Preparation for interview (*See also* Strategy for interview)
  background research, 17
  for broadcast interview, 96–97
  day before in bed, 51
  defining purpose, 16
  "full of subject," 52
  lack of, as fault, 4–5
  for keen reflexes, 51–52
  perfect set of questions, 51
  planning, 18, 51–53
  when unprepared, 90–92
Prepublication review by source, 136–37
Press
  like fish cannery, 75
  power of, 31–32, 88
Press conference, 27, 134–35
"Pressure cooker" interviews, 98
"Pretending information" (*See* Ethics, ploys)
Probe questions, 5, 16, 41–42, 45
Problems of interviewing (*See* Faults of interviewing)
Professional Journalist, The, 23
Profile, personality, 112–13 (*See also* Personality interview)
Prohibitionist as interviewer, 31
Provocations in interviews, 26–27, 36, 44–45
Pseudo events, 26, 82
Public Affairs Information Service Bulletin, 56
Public Broadcast Service, 98
Public officials, as respondents, 4–5, 10, 81–82, 153
Public Opinion, 78
Purpose of interview
  defining, 16, 53–55
  need for, 4
Pursuit in questions (*See* Probe questions)
"Putting words in people's mouths" (*See* Questions, leading, colored)
Pyle, Ernie, 43

Questionnaires, 31, 70, 145
Questions, 34–50, 58–59
  all purpose (*See* Universal questions)
  anecdote soliciting, 45–49, 152
  bomb, 19–20
  on broadcast, 96–98
  like carpenter's tools, 34
  categorized, 35–50
  chronological, 36–37
  colored, 35, 44
  conceptually defining, 40–41
  confronting, 59 (*See also* Confrontation tactics)

Questions (*cont.*)
  convoluted, 6
  creative, 49–50, 117–18
  critical, 26
  direct, 59
  diversionary, 135
  factual, 38–39
  on "feelings," 91, 94
  filter, 38, 59
  first moves, 36
  funnel, 38, 59
  humorous, 36, 38
  hypothetical, 49–50, 117–18
  icebreaker, 11–12, 19, 35–36, 60
  ironic, 38
  leading, 44, 59
  loaded, 59
  naïve, 7
  neutral, 58
  numerically defining, 39–40
  oblique, 59
  opening, 19, 35–36, 97
    first moves, 36
    icebreaker, 11–12, 19, 35, 60
  in personality interview, 119–20
  phrasing, 58–59
  on private thought, 65–66
  probe, 5, 16, 41–42, 45
  quotation soliciting, 42–44
  ridiculous, 117
  sensitive, 19–20, 26–27, 30, 151, 153
  sequence, 60–62
  as strength, 2
  universal, 85–86, 91, 119–20
  when unprepared, 90–92
  "wicked frowns," 15
  writing out, 58
Quiet respondents (*See* Respondents, reluctant)
Quill, The, 70
Quinn, Sally, 23, 65
Quotations
  authentication, 43
  authority, 44
  character revealing, 43
  "dash of spice," 43
  "don't quote me," 153 (*See also* Evasiveness)
  humorous, 43, 68
  figures of speech, 43, 44
  jargon, 43
  "memorable," 124
  notetaking problem, 124, 152
  out of context, 99, 152
  overuse, 43
  recognizing, 42–45
  soliciting, 42–45
  use of, 42–45, 152
  words or meanings, 125

Radio interviewing (*See* Broadcast interviewing)
Rain, in Oregon, 130
Rapists as respondents, 3, 34, 35
Rapport in interviewing
  with bank robber, 34–35

Rapport in interviewing (*cont.*)
  in conceptual questions, 40
  empathy, 23–25
  establishing, 19
  filter questions, affect on, 38
  with interviewers as respondents, 22–23
  when lacking, 26–27
  opening lines of communication, 28–30
  overrapport, 71–72
  research findings, 30, 31–32
  through study of respondent, 58
  with tape recorder, 125–126
Reader's Digest, 70, 73
Reader's Guide to Periodical Literature, 56
Recorders (*See* Tape recorders)
Red Badge of Courage, 114
Redbook, 73
"Redpants," composite, 112
Reed, Rex, 104
Reference Books: A Brief Guide, 57
Reik, Theodor, 24, 116, 116–17
Relaxing in interviews (*See* Rapport)
Reporters and Officials, 88
Reporter's Trade, The, 76–77
Reporting
  as art form, 106 (*See also* New journalism)
  criticisms of, 75–77
  depth, 80–81
  like handline fishing, 75
  informal, 76, 83–85, 87 (*See also* Observation)
  interpretative, 31–32
  on news beats, 75–92
  saturation, 107, 118–19
  team, 80–81
  by telephone, 88–90
  when unprepared, 90–92
  work defined, 77–79
Reporting, 114
Reputation as interviewer, 64, 71
Research for interviewing
  informal, 55–56, 73–74
  library, 56–57
Research on interviewing, 30–33, 55–57
Respondent
  assessing, 57–58
  being interviewed, 139–40
  boring, 138
  bureaucrats, 10, 81–82, 136, 153–54
  coaches, 12
  college students, 13
  ego, 20, 31, 37, 131
  elected officials, 81, 153
  enjoying interview, 11, 24, 30
  evasive, 134
  feeling exploited, 7
  homosexuals, 71
  hostile, 37, 38
  "image" problem, 104–5, 115
  Indians, 71
  inexperienced, 12, 153–54
  intellectuals, 154
  memory problem, 133–34
  new candor, 136
  "nutty people," 154

Respondent (*cont.*)
  police chief, 53–63
  professional journalists, 22–23
  public officials, 10, 45, 81–82, 153
  reasons to deny interview, 17–18
  reasons to give interview, 17
  reluctant, 13, 52, 129–30
  talkative, 52, 62, 97–98
  women, 13–14, 133
  young people, 13, 14
Review of article before publication, 137
Rewards for respondent, 17, 24, 30
Reynolds, Debbie, 136
Rice, Stuart, A., 31
Rockefeller, Nelson, 26
Roethlisberger, F. J., 28
Rogers, Carl R., 28, 29
Rogers, Will, 44
Roosevelt, Theodore, 52, 62
Ross Lillian, 114
Rosson, Ben, 108
Royko, Mike, 23

Salancik, Jerry R., 30, 31–32
Saturation reporting
  defined, 107
  participant observer, 113–14
  scenes dramatized, 115–16
  techniques, 118–19
Saturday Evening Post, 110
Saying Goodbye (*See* Concluding the interview)
Scenes (*See* Detail; Saturation reporting)
School Board Journal, 86
Science and technology news beat, 80
Scott, Vernon, 110
Scripps-Howard chain, 76
Secretaries, as news sources, 83
Seib, Charles B., 77
Selfconfidence, 131
Selfconsciousness, 2, 3, 4
Self-Creations: 13 Impersonalities, 104–5
"Selling" interview request, 18 (*See also* Getting an appointment)
Sensitive questions
  asked arrogantly, 26–27
  asking, 19–20
  in broadcast interviews, 97
  in news reporting, 151, 153
  respondents willing to answer, 30
  "wicked frowns," 15
Sensitivity to feelings, 28–29 (*See also* Nonverbal communication)
Sequence of questions, 60–62
Setting of interview, 11, 32–33, 95
Sex discrimination, interview topic (*See* Policewomen)
Sex research interviewing
  fraudulent, 89
  by Kinsey, Dr. Alfred, 22–23
Short story techniques, 68 (*See also* New Journalism; Anecdotes)
"Show, don't tell," 68, 113, 115 (*See also* New Journalism; Anecdotes)
Shyness, 151 (*See also* Selfconsciousness)
Sigal, Leon V., 88

Silence
  as "question," 34, 45
  selfconsciousness about, 4
  on telephone, 89–90
Silent Messages, 32
Sincerity (*See* Rapport)
Site of interview, 11, 32–33, 95
Sloppy dress, 5
Small talk (*See* Icebreakers; Meeting the respondent)
Smith, Perry, 24
Social amenities, 29 (*See also* Icebreakers)
Socialist as interviewer, 31
Social Science Index, 56
Social science techniques, 3, 30–33
Social welfare news beat, 80
Society page, changes in, 106
Sources (*See also* News beats; Respondents)
  anonymous, 135, 136
  contact with, 76
  for corroboration, 132
  interaction with reporters, 83
  on news béat, 83–85
Southern woman, as "research" topic, 74
Space between conversants, 32–33
Spencer, Murlin, 123
Spikol, Art, 128–29
Spock, Dr. Benjamin, 136
Sports news beat, 80
Springfield, Oregon, 150–54 *passim*
Stages of interview, 11, 16–21
State news beat, 80
Statistics (*See* Questions, numerically defining)
Steffens, Lincoln, 62
Stereotypes, journalistic, 6
Stevens, Leonard, 29, 30
Stevenson, Robert Louis, 61
Stolley, Dick, 106
Storytelling, as interview technique, 46, 72–73 (*See also* Anecdotes)
Strange Case of Dr. Jekyll and Mr. Hyde, The, 61
Strategy, 51–63
  anticipating answers, 59–60
  character assessment, 57–58
  defining purpose, 53–55
  game plan, 60–62
  in multi-interview project, 64–74
  planning questions, 18, 58–59
  requesting appointment, 18, 60–61
  research, 55–57
  varying technique, 62–63
"Strip tease"
  in coverup, 27
  literary, 69
Structure of interview
  chronology, 61
  game plan, 60–62
  GOSS formula, 40–41
  natural curiosity, 61
  ten stages
    discussed, 16–21
    listed, 11
    sample transcript, 11–16

Student apprehensions, 1, 2, 3
Student rebellion, 81
  at Berkeley, 133
Subject of interview (*See* Respondent)
Subterfuges, in reporting 130 (*See also* Ethics)
Suicide on TV, 65
Sunset, 77
Swapping stories, 46, 73 (*See also* Anecdotes)

Taking notes (*See* Notetaking)
Talese, Gay, 113–14, 115–16, 118
Talkative respondents, 52, 62, 97–98
Talking reporters, 30 (*See also* Listening)
Tape Recorders, 104, 125–29, 151, 152
  accessories, 128
  advantages, 125–27
  breakdown, 125, 151
    preventing, 127
  increasing use, 126
  intimidation of respondent, 125–26
  legal considerations, 126, 128–29
  mechanical problems, 125, 127, 151
  mini-recorder, 128
  pocket, 128
  portable, 128
  rapport, affect on, 125–26
  reel-to-reel, 128
  safeguarding tapes, 126
  on telephone, 128–29
  transcribing, 126–27
  types of recorders, 127–28
Taylor, Elizabeth, 23, 51
Team reporting, 80–81
Telephone interviewing, 83–85, 88–90, 129, 151
  with bank robber, 24
  for feature stories, 89
  in fraudulent sex research, 89
  suggestions for use, 89–90
  with tape recorder, 128–29
Telephoning for appointment (*See* Getting an interview)
Television interviewing (*See* Broadcast interviewing)
Television News, 94–95
Television suicide, 65
Ten stages of interview, 11, 16–21 (*See also* Structure of interview)
Terkel, Studs, 9–10, 29, 102, 104, 119, 135, 147, 148
Termination of interview (*See* Concluding the interview)
Texas, 80
Thematic interview, 110
"Third ear," listening with, 116–17 (*See also* Listening)
Thoele, Mike, 134–35
Threats as technique, 130 (*See also* Ethics)
Time, 106
Times Index, The, 57
Tinker, Grant, 110
Tips and tipsters, 72, 81, 87
Today, 98

Top person, interviews with, 54, 71 (*See also* Key people; Sources)
Tough questions (*See* Sensitive questions; Confrontation tactics)
Trading information, 10, 74–75 (*See also* Swapping stories; Anecdotes)
Training for interview, 51–52
Transcribing tapes, 126–27
Transportation news beat, 80
Trickery by interviewer, 29, 139 (*See also* Ethics)
Truth
  checking, 132–33
  encouraging, 28–29
  levels of, 40, 132
  in sex research, 22–23
Twain, Mark, 44, 66
Typewriter, for notes (*See* Notetaking)
Tyrrell, Robert, 26

Uhnak, Dorothy, 57
United Press International, 107
Universal questions
  in news beat coverage, 85–86
  in personality interview, 119–20
  when unprepared, 91
University of Oregon, 93, 99, 144, 150
Unobtrusive Measures, 73
Unpreparedness, 4–5, 90–92
Uses of interviews, 150–54
U.S. Government Periodicals, Index, 57
U.S. News, 108

Vagueness
  in questions, 5
  in respondent, 134
VD investigator, interview with, 140–43
Verbal cues, 31
Vested interest, in respondent, 132
Video display terminal, 125
Voltaire, 2
Voluntary informants, 72, 81, 87

Wallace, Mike, 94, 98
Wall Street Journal Index, 57
Walters, Barbara, 23, 37, 98
Washington, D. C., 56, 59, 89
Washington, D. C. coverage, 76–77
Washingtonian, 53
Washington Post, 23, 65, 77, 136
Watergate scandal, 136
Watson, Dr., 66
Weathermen underground, 107
Webb, Eugene J., 30, 31–32, 73
Welch, Raquel, 48, 49
WGN radio, 24–25
Whitman, Alden, 105
Who-what-when-where-why-how, 38–39
"Why?" (*See* Conceptually defining questions)
Wilde, Oscar, 44
Wiretap laws, 129
Wissbeck, Larry, 94, 96
Witness reliability, 64, 134
Wolf, Jeanne, 98, 133
Wolfe, Tom, 106, 107, 115, 118, 119
Women in Law Enforcement, 57
Women in Policing, 57
Women as respondents, 13, 14, 133
Women's Studies Abstracts, 56
Woodward, Bob, 136
Working, 29, 104, 135, 148
Work of the Television Journalist, The, 26
Writer's Digest, 104, 128–29
Writer's Digest Handbook of Article Writing, 105
Writing in Style, 65
Writing out questions, 58

Young people as respondents, 13, 14

Zimbalist, Ephrem, Jr., 36
Zolotow, Maurice, 105, 115
Zunin, Leonard, 19
Zunin, Natalie, 19